# Teaching the Way
## Jesus, the Early Church and Today

Joseph A. Grassi

UNIVERSITY
PRESS OF
AMERICA

Copyright © 1982 by

**University Press of America, Inc.**

Copyright 1978 by St. Mary's College Press,

**P.O. Box 19101, Washington, D.C. 20036**

**Library of Congress Cataloging in Publication Data**

Grassi, Joseph A.
   Teaching the way.

   Rev. ed. of: Jesus as teacher. 1978.
   Includes bibliographical references.
   1. Christian education--History. 2. Jesus Christ--
Teaching methods. 3. Education--History. I. Title.
BV1465.G7   1982       207           82-7054
ISBN 0-8191-2501-6                    AACR2
ISBN 0-8191-2502-4 (pbk.)

Scriptural quotations are from *The New
American Bible*, copyright ©1970 by the Con-
fraternity of Christian Doctrine, Washington,
D.C.

# Contents

Part IV
# The Teacher in the New Testament and the Teacher Today

# Introduction

In recent years, for a variety of reasons, the process of Christian formation has become a matter of concern, not only to priests, ministers, and teachers, but also to "ordinary" church members as well as high school and college students. At the same time the realization is spreading that the question is not simply: "How can we most effectively hand on the Faith to the next generation?" It is rather how we can have a much more dynamic appreciation of the life-style of Jesus and the early church that could have practical application in the world of today.

The purpose of this book, then, is to bring the light of the New Testament to bear on this vital question. As a result we will study how to "teach as Jesus did," and also learn in the same way that his disciples and the early church learned. This book, then, is a study of Jesus as a Teacher: how he taught, and how others learned from him and passed on this tradition.

Part I provides the necessary background, describing first-century Jewish and Greek models of teaching. Part II is devoted to what the gospels tell us about Jesus as a teacher. Part III then considers the information in the remaining New Testament as to how teaching was carried on in the early church. And Part IV proposes some conclusions to be drawn from these models for effective Christian teaching and learning today.

This book is a revised and expanded edition of *Jesus as Teacher* published by St. Mary's Press in 1978. It has an additional chapter entitled "The Gnostic View of Jesus and the Teacher Today." It is hoped that this new edition by University Press will make the book available to an even wider audience of teachers, clergy and concerned Christians as well as to increased use as a college, or advanced high school text.

# Part I

# Teaching Models in the First Century

# 1. The Jewish Family

For a Jew of the first century, religious education meant study of the *Torah*. This word is not accurately translated by "law." The *Torah* was not only a system of rules but, more importantly, a whole way of life that had to be learned through close association with a teacher. "Religious observances" would be a better, though still not complete, translation. Part of the *Torah* included all the laws in regard to ethical behavior found in the Bible, beginning with the Ten Commandments. These were continually brought up to date by being applied to new situations through the oral instruction of Jewish teachers. Other rules of the *Torah* concerned religious customs such as observance of the Sabbath and of feasts, along with prayers and blessings that were to be recited at various times during the day. These rules also entered into the hundreds of details of daily life such as the foods that might be eaten and the clothing that could be worn. All these laws and observances were looked upon not as a legalistic system but as *ways of remembering God* in the midst of busy everyday life. Further, these laws of the *Torah* were a discipline which required an intense awareness of the importance of ordering one's entire life in the path of God. Finally, the *Torah* was a "fence" or protection that kept the Jews' religion intact in the face of constant pressure to conform to the customs and practices of the surrounding Greek world in which they lived.

The first and most important setting for religious education was the Jewish family. Any further instruction was considered an extension and continuation of what was begun at home. The education in the family was by no means theoretical; it was based on active imitation of the religious behavior of parents both at home and in public.

The book of Proverbs, probably compiled in the early part of the fifth century B.C., states that true learning begins with imitating one's parents (1:8-9). And Ben Sirach, writing in the second century B.C., says that the greatest reward for a father is to see a son grow up imitating him in such a way that, "At the father's death, he will not seem dead, since he leaves after him one like himself" (30:4).

The Law itself strongly reinforced this imitative teaching approach and, in fact, made it a sacred obligation. In the view of the Old Testament, the study of religion was a "study" of God's wonderful acts. God's acts were to be gratefully acknowledged and recounted from father to son. Accordingly, God told Moses that the great signs in Israel's history were to be told to sons and grandsons as a precious heritage (Exod. 10:1-2). The formative events of Israel were not mere memories from the past but living experiences of faith and liberation that each generation should share and relive with the next: "Take care and be earnestly on your guard not to forget the things which your own eyes have seen, nor let them slip from your memory as long as you live, but teach them to your children and to your children's children" (Deut. 4:9).

The central prayer of Israel was the daily *shemah*: "Hear O Israel! The Lord is our God, the Lord alone! Therefore, you shall love the Lord, your God, with all your heart, and with all your soul and with all your strength" (Deut. 6:4-5). Every Israelite learned this *shemah* by repeating it after his parents at home and by constant reminders: "Take to heart these words which I enjoin on you today. Drill them into your children. Speak of them at home and abroad, whether you are busy or at rest. Bind them at your wrist as a sign and let them be as a pendant on your forehead. Write them on the doorposts of your houses and on your gates" (Deut. 6:6-9).

The *Torah* itself had a strong didactic purpose: it was meant to recall to Israel, especially to children, the meaning of their special call by God: "Later on, when your son asks you what these ordinances, statutes and decrees mean which the Lord, our God, has enjoined on you, you shall say to your son, 'We were slaves of Pharaoh in Egypt, but the Lord brought us out of Egypt with his strong hand . . .'" (Deut. 6:20-21). No doubt a child would ask such questions of his father many times in the course of family observances of the Law. For example, when the first-born animals were presented to the Lord, a son would ask, "What does this mean?" (Exod 13:14). The response of the father would be that God had delivered the first-born of Israel from the great plague that had killed all the first-born in Egypt (Exod. 13:14-16).

The most vivid and unforgettable occasions for this "family-centered learning" were when the whole family participated together in the great religious feasts. The Passover ceremony, even today, is meant to be a form of "live teaching." The ritual directs the youngest child to ask the father during the ceremony, "What does this rite of yours mean?" (Exod. 12:26). The father then explains, "This is the Passover sacrifice of the Lord . . ." (Exod. 12:27). Before the Passover meal, a diligent search of the whole house is carried out by parents and children in order to remove carefully all leavened bread. This unusual action also would occasion questions by the children. Once again the father is directed to explain: "On this day you shall explain to your son, 'This is because of what the Lord did for me when I came out of Egypt'" (Exod. 13:8). A more detailed explanation would follow telling how the Israelites had to leave Egypt so quickly that they did not have time to put leaven into the dough that was being readied for baking.

In fact, religious feasts were designed so as to be "multi-media" presentations that could not easily be forgotten. For example, during the Feast of Tents or Tabernacles, when families came to Jerusalem for the fall harvest festival, each household built tents or booths out of leafy branches and lived outdoors during the seven days of the feast. Thus, each household recalled that they were a pilgrim people and had lived in tents when God brought them out of Egypt. A child could hardly forget when he learned from his parents through such active involvement and participation.

Yet the education of children was not something that took place only during these special, extraordinary events of each year. The daily family prayer, the *shemah*, and the weekly Sabbath were the center of family life. The observance of the Sabbath was governed by many practices involving each member of the family. The whole family celebrated the opening of the Sabbath by a special meal together after sunset on Friday. The important goal of the Sabbath, as well as of all other religious laws, was to *remember* — by re-presenting in the most vivid way possible — what God had done for them, his people.

To sum up: *Religious teaching began in the home through imitation of parents. A living model was required for imitation because a whole way of life, a whole way of doing things was to be learned. Jewish children had to learn what God had done and* was doing for them now. *They acquired this knowledge through total participation in family religious life. Teachers coming into the Jewish child's later life were regarded almost as second parents from whom the older child could likewise learn by means of imitation. Thus in both Proverbs and Sirach the writers frequently address their readers as "my son," (e.g., Prov. 1:8, 2:1, 3:1, Sir. 21:1).*

# 2. The Pharisees and Essenes

The party of the Pharisees could justly be called the "cream of Judaism" at the time of Jesus. The ordinary people looked up to them as their religious leaders. Consequently, their teaching practices are very important for our study. The Pharisees appear on almost every page of the gospels as the antagonists of Jesus. Yet some of this polemic may reflect tensions *within* the church, as well as *between* the church and Judaism at the time the gospels were written, rather than those between Jesus and the Jews of his time.[1] In fact, there are hints that Jesus himself was closely linked to the Pharisees. The Gospel of Luke recalls that Jesus sometimes ate in their homes (11:37; 14:1). The accusation of eating with unwashed hands was directed to Jesus' disciples, not to Jesus himself (Mark 7:2). Many early Christian converts came from the Pharisees (Acts 15:5; 23:6-9).

Every Pharisee was one of the scribes, that is, a man especially trained as an expert in the *Torah*. After the required period of preparation, he could be authorized as an official interpreter of the Law. The most distinguished position of the day was that of a scribe. He wore a special long robe and was always given a seat of honor at public gatherings, such as in the synagogue, in the marketplace, and at weddings (Matt. 23:6-7). Indeed, the common people looked up to scribes not only as authorized interpreters of the *Torah*, but as living models to be followed.

The Pharisees themselves were distinguished by a most perfect observance of the Law, even going so far as to apply all the priestly laws of ritual cleanness to laymen. They formed a closed society open to membership only on the part of those who were meticulous observers of the *Torah*. They had regular meetings together. Those who wished to join them had to go through a strict "novitiate" before they could be approved as full members.[2]

For the scribe or Pharisee, the most important matter in his education was the *Torah*. Since this was a whole way of life that had to be learned from living examples, the essential matter was to "get yourself a teacher" (*Aboth* 1:6,16).[3] Because of the vital importance of oral instruction and imitation of the living teacher, written texts, except for the Scriptures, were not used.[4] In contrast to mere theoretical knowledge, the constant stress was on "doing". Close to the time of Jesus, the Rabbi Shammai used to say, "Make the *Torah* a fixed duty; say little, and do much" (*Aboth* 1:15).

The transmission of the *Torah* was not merely a matter of handing down a fixed body of tradition in oral form. The essential point was the succession of living teachers (from the time of Moses, as they thought) who embodied this tradition and lived it out in their lives. For this reason, the Pharisee teachers pointed back with pride to a genealogy of teachers from whom they had learned. Within this general tradition there were various schools such as the school of Shammai, and the school of Hillel. Here, again, it was a question not of institutions or buildings but of a certain "living school" which followed a traditional life-style that went back to Shammai or Hillel.

Because of the importance of imitation, disciples spent a great deal of time with their teacher in his home, following him in the street and accompanying him in his work. At all times they carefully observed what he did and listened to his words. In fact, the Jewish Fathers advised that as much time as possible should be spent with wise men: "Let your house be a meeting place for wise men, cover yourself with the dust of their feet (by constantly following them) and drink in their words with thirst" (*Aboth* 1:4).

However, the student was not expected to be a mere "rubber-stamp" of his teacher, or a "sponge-type" who just absorbed the words of the master without discretion. The teacher expected him to ask intelligent questions and to probe for the reasons behind his words. *Pîrkē Aboth* ("The Sayings of the Fathers") illustrates this by the following passage: "There are four types of pupils of the wise men: a sponge, a funnel, a strainer, and a sieve. A sponge which absorbs everything; a funnel, which lets in at one end and out of the other; a strainer which lets the wine pass and retains the sediment; a sieve which lets out the bran dust and retains the fine flour" (*Aboth* 5:18).

Creative ability was also encouraged; a good student was supposed to *add* to his instructor's words. It was said that there were forty-eight qualities of a good student of the *Torah*. One of these was that "he asks and answers; he listens and adds to his learning" (*Aboth* 6:6). Hillel, the great rabbi who was a contemporary of Jesus, used to say, "Whoever makes his name great loses his name, and whoever does not add makes to cease" (*Aboth* 1:13). This saying was understood in reference to original contributions on the part of pupils.

It is important to note that teaching was not just an individual matter. The disciple learned as a member of a small community associated with the teacher. The next important step after finding a teacher was to "get yourself a companion" (*Aboth* 1:6). Learning could not take place in isolation. A saying of Hillel was, "Sever yourself not from the congregation" (*Aboth* 2:5). The Pharisees took this dictum to heart. They were a very close association of friends with their own regulations and frequent meetings that took place during a fellowship meal especially on the Friday evening before the Sabbath.

Such learning through friends and companions had a strong tradition behind it. The forty-eight qualities referred to above particularly mention fellowship with colleagues as an important factor in learning. A friend of this kind should be honored just as one's teacher: "Let your student's honor be as dear to you as your own; let the honor of your friend be as dear as the reverence due your teacher; and let the reverence due your teacher be as dear as the reverence due to heaven" (*Aboth* 4:15).

To sum up thus far: *For the scribes and Pharisees, the all-important matter was the learning of the* Torah *which entailed a whole manner of life. It was to be learned in intimate association with a teacher and by careful imitation of his actions and life. It supposed also a community of "scholars" who would be learning companions.*

The "monks" of Qumran, often identified with the Essenes, were an unusual Jewish community who lived in buildings and caves near the Dead Sea. Their recently found scrolls have brought us much exciting new knowledge about Jewish life at the time of Jesus. The members dedicated themselves by oath to perfect observance of every detail of the *Torah*. They formed a commune, sharing all their personal properties and making decisions by vote concerning matters that affected them all. They would have nothing to do with the Temple priests because they did not regard them as true priests. The group was so zealous in regard to the Law, especially the precepts about the poor, that they devoted two days' income each month to the needy of Israel outside their gates. Their community rule yields important information concerning religious education in the *Torah*.

A candidate for admission was placed under the special care of an overseer who would "enlighten him in regard to all the laws of the community" (*Qumran Rule* 6:15). This would take place during a two-year period, during which the novice would be expected to progress under the guidance and example of his teacher. After this probation period he received his rank as a full member of the community. Upon entry, he was required to take an oath to follow the law of Moses with his whole heart and soul. This promise was made in the presence of the whole community who renewed their own vows at the same time. The zeal of the community was such that they studied the Law on a twenty-four hour basis. In order to do this, a number of them worked in three eight-hour shifts.

The Essenes ate together, prayed as a community, shared their possessions, and deliberated as a body. Their teaching example was the community Guardian. He was looked upon as a true spiritual father. The *Damascus Document* directed him to show the community the same love and compassion that a father has toward his own children (*Rule* 13:9). If any of the members strayed from the true path of the Law, he was to bring them back as a shepherd seeks his lost sheep. He was to see to it that no one was oppressed or crushed (13:9-10). In this way, the learning process, begun through guidance and imitation, was to continue. Each person's progress was reviewed yearly.

In addition, a great deal of active learning took place through personal contacts. The members were enjoined to "love each man his brother as himself, and extend their hands to help the poor, the needy, and the stranger" (*Rule* 6). This took a very practical form in the injunction to speak honestly to a fellow member if he failed in the Law. The warning was to be given in humility and charity on the very day the transgression occurred. No one was to bring a matter to the entire congregation unless the person concerned was advised, first privately and then before two witnesses (*Rule*, 5 and 6). The procedure reminds us of Matt. 18:15-18 and the concern of the church for the brother who has gone astray.

We see then, by way of summary: *The community of Qumran attached great importance to teaching in the form of personal guidance under the supervision of a master who would guide first the novice then the full member in the way of life which was the* Torah. *The teacher's work was reinforced by the strong brotherly obligation that the "monks" felt to help and encourage one another.*

# 3. Philo and Josephus

Philo was a contemporary of Jesus, living in the Greek atmosphere of Alexandria in Egypt. Unfortunately, we have little direct information about his Jewish training, but he does give us considerable information about his Hellenistic education. He is especially concerned about the relationship between Greek education and virtue. He sees knowledge as remaining in the purely theoretical realm unless it is combined with practice and virtue.

According to Philo, a student acquires virtue by imitating good men. He uses Abraham as a model and ideal of learning, noting that Abraham directed his attention not to what was said but to those who were saying it, and then he imitated their life.[5] Jacob also is not a mere listener but an imitator of persons' lives.[6] Philo has a problem in reconciling Greek education with virtue, but his Jewish background no doubt helped him to understand that personal religious formation needed live human examples to follow.

Josephus, the Jewish historian, was born about the time of Jesus' death. While his references are brief, they provide us with valuable additions to our picture of Jewish education in the first century. In his *Life,*[7] Josephus tells us that when he was sixteen years old, he decided to make a trial of the three main Jewish sects of the time: the Pharisees, the Sadducees, and the Essenes. In this process he spent a number of years living in the desert with a hermit called Banus. Here his principal concern was to imitate his teacher's way of life. Then he returned to Jerusalem and remained with the Pharisees, observing their conduct and way of life. It is of special interest here that he attaches great importance to the fact that he was a disciple of a holy man and imitated him.

In his work, *Against Apion*, Josephus defends Jewish history and practice against those who had attacked its truthfulness and value. In regard to the Law, he affirms that Jewish children are taught the exercise of the Law and the deeds of their ancestors *in order to imitate them.*[8] He describes Moses as a teacher who was concerned not merely with instruction but with a whole manner of life.[9] For this reason he concludes at the end of his book that the *Torah* does not depend on words, but on persons' actions. By making these "words" part of their life, Jews become teachers of other men.

To sum up briefly: *We have seen that both Philo and Josephus see the teacher as a person to be imitated as well as listened to. True learning is contagious—it is learned through actual contact with holy men and women.*

# 4. Greek Models of the Teacher

Greek ideals of education had a strong influence not only on the scattered Jewish communities outside Palestine (the Diaspora) but even on Jerusalem itself. The early Gentile converts whom Paul brought into the church were people imbued with Hellenistic culture. These neophytes placed a strong Greek stamp on the early churches.

In classical Greece,[10] the relationship between teacher and male student was looked upon as one of the highest and closest bonds of love. It was an affectionate relationship that might easily be misunderstood if the total context of this love were not seen. The beginnings of this close relationship lay in a society that was originally very military-minded and, hence, male-oriented. The schools were especially concerned with preparing young men to meet military requirements. Teachers presented military heroes of the past and present as patterns for their pupils to imitate. This was not merely because of their prowess in battle but mainly because of their outstanding virtue.

The love relationship between master and disciple went far beyond the realm of physical love, or sensual desire: it involved a deep aspiration on the part of the student to imitate an ideal of excellence that he found in his teacher. On the part of the older man there was a desire not only to gain the young man's affection but also to be a model that his student could look up to. The teacher regarded himself as a spiritual father, a father who should be creative and self-giving. While the lover-beloved aspect was never absent, the total relationship was based on what the Greeks would consider the highest ideals.

Our principal concern is with the Hellenistic age beginning with the conquest of Alexander the Great (c. 333 B.C.) and continuing into the New Testament period and beyond. Alexander played a key role in extending Greek culture and influence over most of the world, including Palestine. The ideal of Greek education in this period was the formation of the whole man. In this total formation religious-moral considerations were prominent. The child, after his home training, began his primary education at the age of seven and continued to about fourteen. As in all Greek education, there was a strong emphasis on physical education in the form of bodily training through sports.

In the "primary" school, the basic elements of reading and writing were taught. The primary teacher was not held in much esteem, since he only taught the rudiments of knowledge. The all-important person for the training of the child was the "pedagogue," *paidōgogos*. He was a specially selected, usually well-educated slave who accompanied the boy to school, monitored him in his study, and helped form his whole character through moral education. The student learned through the constant companionship, example, and help of the pedagogue.

"Secondary" education began at fourteen and continued to about twenty-one. Here the young man began to study the Greek classics. He also had instruction in the arts, especially music, along with mathematics, science, and astronomy. The aim in studying the classics was not merely that of understanding their grammar and style but of appreciating the moral teaching, especially the heroic examples of the great men of literature. The classical Greek ideal of the love relationship between master and pupil continued to play an important part throughout this education. This period of education came to a close with one year of special training in the *Ephebē*, which was a school of preparation for military and civic service.

Next came the "university," or higher training in rhetoric or philosophy, which was considered the most important part of education and was restricted to a well-to-do minority. Other service-oriented professions, such as medicine, were learned through a type of "in-service" training. The medical student, after a few days of fundamental lectures, would attach himself to a physician as his teacher. He would accompany him on his calls and learn through actual observation and practice. When he had learned enough, he became an assistant, then an associate, of the doctor.

In university education, the study of rhetoric centered on oratory.

This was to enable a student to assume the important roles of politician, lawyer, teacher, or other professions in which skill in oral communication was essential. Here also the principle of personal relationship between teacher and pupil was considered very important. Groups of students clustered about a master so much that they were frequently referred to as his band or *chorus*. There was also a deep spiritual and fraternal bond between the pupils of the same teacher.

Higher education in philosophy had no resemblance to the academic study of philosophy today. Philosophers were small bands of intellectual élite who broke away from the usual culture around them. To "study philosophy" meant to adopt a new way of life under the guidance and example of a teacher. Philosophers could be recognized in any crowd by their special dress and manner of living. The Cynics, for example, were the "hippies" of their day. They wore very rough clothes, or rags, and were "dropouts" from society. They symbolized their break from society by ignoring the usual conventions; they wore long hair, rarely washed, and begged from people to show they had broken from "polite society."

It was in the schools of philosophy that the personal character of Greek education was most clearly witnessed. The philosopher was not just an academic teacher. He was also expected to be a warm companion and guide. He lived together with his disciples in a type of commune. His words were of only minor importance in comparison with his actions and way of life which were to be imitated by his students. Here again, a deep bond of affection was forged between teacher and disciples as well as between fellow-disciples of the same master.

To sum up: *The Greek view of educaton was very close to the Semitic one. In fact, due to the interaction between the two cultures, it is very difficult to separate them. Both recognized the importance of learning through imitation of a teacher in a community. This view had an important influence on Jesus and the early church. In the coming chapters, we will see how New Testament teaching develops along the same personal patterns.*

# Part II

# Jesus the Teacher

In Part I, we have studied teaching models in the first century in the Jewish family, and in Jewish and Greek teachers. We have seen that the whole emphasis is on the teacher as a concrete embodiment of what is taught. The teacher's own life is meant to be a model for the student. In Part II, we will study the teaching approach of Jesus. He continues the Jewish and Greek tradition of the teacher as a model for the disciple but gives it new dimensions. Moreover, Jesus teaches by sharing his own mission, powers, and unique personal insights with his followers. Imitation of Jesus is not only imitation of his human personal actions, but an imitation and sharing of the powerful love of God working through him.

# 5. In the Company of Jesus: the Traveling Commune

In reading through the gospels, nothing strikes the reader more forcibly than the image of Jesus as a *teacher*. The title *didaskalos* or "teacher" is that most commonly given him; it appears some forty-eight times in the four gospels. The evangelists likewise predominantly describe his activity in terms of the verb *didaskein*, "to teach" (some fifty times). Although Jesus frequently taught in the formal setting of the synagogue, most of his time was spent as a traveling teacher whose students followed him wherever he went. Jesus had a peripatetic school: he taught in the open air on the mount of beatitudes (Matt. 5:1-2); on the seashore (Mark 4:1); in the temple area (Mark 11:17).

Here we are particularly concerned with how Jesus actually trained and formed his disciples. The principal impact of his teaching was felt by a small group who remained in Jesus' constant company, working with him and imitating his life-style. These disciples formed a definite and identifiable group. Jesus named twelve as his companions whom he would send to preach the good news (Mark 3:14).

The gospel of Mark does not clearly indicate that anyone outside the Twelve had the title of disciple. This may show that, originally, only the Twelve were Jesus' disciples. In Matthew, Luke, and John, the number of disciples becomes expanded beyond twelve. This, however, may be influenced[11] by the actual situation in the church at the time the gospels were written. It is significant that Luke, when it comes to choosing a new apostle to take Judas' place, notes the following qualification: the man chosen must be someone who was in Jesus' constant company right from the time of John the Baptist (Acts 1:21-22).

The disciples of Jesus were not with him in a merely passive role but as active collaborators sharing the same mission and powers as Jesus himself: "He named twelve as his companions whom he would send to preach the good news; they were likewise to have authority to expel demons!" (Mark 3:14-15). Jesus felt called to go out and search for people in order to call them to repentance in view of the coming kingdom. He was to be a "fisher of men." When he calls his disciples it is to invite them to follow him in the same mission: "Come after me; I will make you fishers of men" (Mark 1:17). This invitation to share his own life work comes directly after the first missionary tour of Jesus when he went through Galilee announcing, "This is the time of fulfilment. The Reign of God is at hand! Reform your lives and believe in the gospel!" (Mark 1:15). The sequence brings out the idea that the Twelve are to share the same work.

Jesus' little group could be called a traveling commune. Like the monks at Qumran, they shared their possessions and had a common purse (John 12:6). Likewise they shared what they had with the poor outside their number: for example, during the Last Supper, when Judas left, the others assumed that he had gone out to give something to the poor in the name of the community (John 13:29). Such a closely knit group provided ample opportunity to learn not only from Jesus but from one another. The gospels record some of their discussions, which at times became so heated that Jesus had to intervene—for example, the argument among the disciples as to who would be greatest in the kingdom. With his characteristic deep insight, Jesus knew this was happening. So he called the group together and spoke to them: "'If anyone wishes to rank first, he must remain the last one of all and the servant of all.' Then he took a little child, stood him in their midst, and putting his arms around him, said to them, 'Whoever welcomes a child such as this for my sake welcomes me. And whoever welcomes me welcomes, not me, but him who sent me'" (Mark 9:35-37).

From the beginning there was something unique in Jesus' bond with his disciples. It was based on a friendship that resulted from a special choice. There was nothing casual in the way that Jesus' disciples came to him. In those days, it was customary for a disciple to choose his teacher.

However, Jesus reversed the process and went out to choose his disciples. Jesus had in mind this special love of choice and initiative when he said, "It was not you who chose me, it was I who chose you to go forth and bear fruit" (John 15:16).

In choosing his disciples, Jesus presented them with a new challenge and vast responsibility in the kingdom of God—as traveling messengers and agents of God. In those days a disciple was in a definitely subordinate relationship to a master; he was obliged to serve him in many little ways as a recompense for his studies. For example, disciples customarily opened a way before their teacher going through a crowd, or helped him put on his sandals. Jesus permitted nothing of this kind. On the contrary, he invited persons into a new type of dynamic discipleship. To be a disciple meant to share equally with him an urgent mission to the world. Jesus summed up the meaning of this friendship and sharing between equals when he said, 'I no longer speak of you as slaves, for a slave does not know what his master is about. Instead, I call you friends, since I have made known to you all that I heard from my Father" (John 15:15).

Especially striking is Jesus' trust in these men and his ability patiently to allow them to learn by their mistakes. James and John had to be warned about their need for forbearance when they were highly indignant about the lack of hospitality in Samaria: "When his disciples James and John saw this, they said, 'Lord would you not have us call down fire from heaven to destroy them?' He turned toward them only to reprimand them" (Luke 9:54-55). Peter had to be publicly rebuked for his poor understanding of Jesus' type of leadership (Mark 8:33). The Twelve had to be warned, perhaps often, that they were not to assume the role of leadership in a worldly sense (Mark 10:41-45). The ultimate in trust was Jesus' refusal to abandon hope in Peter even after he fled at the time of Jesus' arrest and publicly denied that he even knew him (Mark 14:30; 14:66-72).

To sum up: *Jesus' approach to teaching was unique for his time. His "students" were not passive listeners but active collaborators, sharing everything the master had. Jesus' disciples were a traveling commune in the continual company of the master. Thus they were able to learn di-*

*rectly by imitation and example. The essential ingredients in Jesus' approach were friendship, love, and trust. Jesus knew they had to learn from experience and mistakes. He was willing to forgive and wait for them to learn through the ups and downs of everyday life.*

# 6. Jesus' Basic Insight and Life-Style

To study Jesus as a teacher we must first have an accurate picture of what he was truly like, and to gain such a picture is not easy. Biblical scholarship has taught us that the gospels are confessional documents. They were written *for* the church as well as *by* the church to tell the good news of the saving event of God's intervention in history through Jesus Christ—especially by Jesus' death, resurrection, and exaltation. The gospels were not written primarily to give us a biography of the earthly Jesus.

Nonetheless, the church has always believed that the Jesus of history and the Jesus of faith are to be identified and that neither can stand alone. So while it is difficult, indeed impossible, to find a detailed history of Jesus' earthly life, modern study of the gospels is able to furnish a new perspective on Jesus' life-style that can be meaningful to people today.

If we fully want to know another person, we try to find out his or her primary motivation and his or her basic direction in life: what is this person really after? In reading the gospels, there is nothing that is so evident as the Jewishness of Jesus. He was born of a Jewish mother, circumcized the eighth day like all other Jewish boys as a sign of his incorporation into the covenant of Israel, the people of God. Every page of the gospels shows how he tried to identify himself with his people and to bring to realization their highest hopes and ideals.

The most notable aspiration of Israel was to be truly God's son in the way that the Lord wanted his people to be. The title "Son of God" was the most prized possession of Israel. When God spoke to Moses, he ordered him to say to Pharaoh, "Israel is my son, my first born . . . let my son go, that he may serve me" (Exod. 4:22-23). In the future expectations of Israel, a day would come when Israel would truly understand this title and become sons of God in a sense far beyond anything they could dream of: "Whereas they were called 'Lo-ammi,' (that is, 'Not my people'), They shall be called, 'Children of the living God'" (Hos. 3:(2):1).

Is there any way of knowing whether Jesus himself thought in terms of fulfilling Israel's destiny as God's son? We cannot read the mind of Jesus. Yet Matthew's account of Jesus' baptism gives us reason to believe that at least the evangelist, if not Jesus himself, thought so. It has been pointed out[12] that the baptismal words, "This is my beloved Son. My favor rests on him" (Matt. 3:17), are a remarkable parallel to the words of God to Moses, "Israel is my son, my first born" (Exod. 4:22). The saying is in the third person in both Exodus and Matthew. So Jesus himself very probably at some time became aware that as a true Israelite he could bring to full meaning in himself the title "Son of God."

The fourth gospel provides a saying of Jesus that many scholars believe belongs to a primitive core of Jesus' own words: "I solemnly assure you, the Son cannot do anything by himself—he can only do what he sees the Father doing. For whatever the Father does, the Son does likewise. For the Father loves the Son and everything the Father does he shows him" (John 5:19-20).

The saying above has its root in an ancient proverb used by craftsmen at that time. As was pointed out earlier, a young man learned his future trade or profession from his father. If a father, for example, was a carpenter, the son would be a carpenter also. His trade school would be his father's workshop. The picture, then, is that of a loving father anxious to show his son all the secrets of the trade. And on the other side, a young son is carefully watching and imitating his father so he also can become a skilled craftsman. The whole process would not be passive watching but active participation. The son would have his own tools and follow his father step by step.

With this in mind, it is easy to picture Jesus working in the carpenter shop of Joseph his father. As a boy he would be looking intently at his father, copying his work. Joseph, on the other hand, would be the craftsman-teacher lovingly showing his son all that he knows. In this setting, we see how natural it was for people to say, "Isn't this the carpenter's son?" (Matt. 13:55).

May it not have been in this context that Jesus reflected deeply on the familiar craftsman's proverb, "The son does nothing except what he sees his father doing"? If this was true of earthly fathers and sons, should it not be true of the heavenly Father also? Should not a true son of God be one who watches and imitates God the Father? Here, then, would be the secret of a true son of God. (The Semitic expression "son of" carries a much deeper sense of imitation than the English expression which mainly deals with identification. A "son of thunder" in the Semitic sense — in Mark 3:17, James and John are called "sons of thunder" — would be a forceful, dynamic, impulsive person. A "son of light" is a light-filled person; while a "son of darkness" is one who follows the works of darkness).

For us today, the idea of "imitating God" seems quite far-fetched, influenced as we are by philosophical reflections on God. For the Hebrew, however, God was always manifesting himself to persons both in nature and in history, where he was continually involved in human affairs. The Scriptures were a precious record of this God of history, bringing out the characteristic pattern of his action. The way he acted in the past was so typical of his present action that Scripture was considered as the Word of God addressing people in their present concrete situation.

Jesus, then, would turn to Scripture as a model for his imitation of the Father. Of all Scripture the most important part was the history of the formation of the covenant relationship between God and his people. This was the result of God's own loving initiative. It is briefly yet powerfully described in the prologue to the Decalogue: "I, the Lord, am your God, who brought you out of the land of Egypt, that place of slavery" (Exod. 20:2). In other words, when the Israelite people were living in bondage and slavery, with no prospects of human freedom, God himself took the first step to free them. He was truly a liberating Person who went out to those who were in need, at a time when they were helpless. For Jesus, this was the root of the covenant; it was *grace* — God's covenant love — that made him take the first step in liberating his people. This would be Jesus' own basic model: if God himself was a God of grace, offering love and freedom, this must be his way also—he must take the first step in going out to those in need and bondage. Nowhere will we find Jesus precisely saying that his motto was the prologue to the commandments. However, his actions and revolutionary approach to people, in contrast to that of other religious leaders of his time such as the Pharisees and Qumran community, show that this must have been the case. This important point will be illustrated later. First, let us give some concrete illustrations of Jesus' ideal of imitating the Father in this aspect of grace, initiative, and unconditional love.

Jesus likened himself to a good shepherd who goes out to search for the lost and abandoned (Matt. 18:12-14; Luke 15:3-7; John 10:11-18). This image of the good shepherd is modeled on that of God himself as described by Ezekiel the prophet, chapter 34. Here God contrasts his own leadership to that of human leaders (shepherds). The human shepherd actually is providing for himself, not the sheep. He wants their milk and meat for his nourishment; he wants to shear their wool to cover his shoulders (34:1-3). God, however, is primarily concerned about the sheep themselves; he brings them to the best pasture; he goes out to seek for the lost, the wounded, the abandoned: "For thus says the Lord God: I myself will look after and tend my sheep. As a shepherd tends his flock when he finds himself among his scattered sheep, so will I tend my sheep. I will rescue them from every place where they were scattered when it was cloudy and dark" (34:11-12). "I myself will pasture my sheep; I myself will give them rest, says the Lord God. The lost I will seek out, the strayed I will bring back, the injured I will bind up, the sick I will heal . . ." (34:15-16).

When Jesus spoke of himself as the good shepherd, he gave an example of grace in action, the root of the covenant. Who were the lost, the abandoned, the unwanted of his time? To imitate the Father, he must take the first step toward them. These people were those who for various reasons felt ostracized socially and religiously from the community—for example, the sick, especially those mentally ill, who were considered to be possessed by devils and carrying the burden of hidden sins. Those with notable physical deformities, such as lepers, the lame and blind, could not take part in religious worship in the temple and often were socially ostracized as well. Also the "tax collectors and sinners" were people whose occupations made them outcasts to be avoided. Women also were regarded by most men of the time as a socially and religiously inferior class. And, of course, the Gentile or non-Jew was detested by many people as an unwanted intruder in the land.

We might look at Jesus' approach and initiative to the "outcasts" of Israel—first of all, to the "tax collectors and sinners." The designation "sinner" was not only given to people who actually broke the Jewish Law. It was also an epithet for all those whose very occupation or business made people suspect that they were not careful observers of Jewish Law. Jesus had the reputation of frequently associating with such people. He was accused of being their special friend: "The Son of Man appeared eating and drinking, and they say, 'This one is a glutton and drunkard, a lover of tax collectors and those outside the law!'" (Matt. 11:19). Indeed, this group of "outcasts" seemed especially attracted to Jesus: "Tax collectors and those known as sinners came to join Jesus and his disciples at dinner. The Pharisees saw this and complained to the disciples, 'What reason can the Teacher have for eating with tax collectors and those who disregard the law?'" (Matt. 9:10-11).

Today, of course, the occupations of tax collectors, or respectable IRS agents, are at least acceptable, if not very appealing. In the time of Jesus, however, no respectable and pious Jew would associate with tax collectors because they were regarded as friends and agents of the hated Roman rulers—close associates of Gentiles whom most Jews avoided as a matter of course. In addition, tax collectors often bought their office from the Romans and made extra money on the side by charging exorbitant amounts to the ordinary people.

Many people, then, were deeply shocked by Jesus' actually going to a tax collector's office and choosing a tax official to be one of the twelve men constantly in his company: "As he moved on he saw Levi the son of Alphaeus at his tax collector's post, and said to him, 'Follow me.' Levi got up and became his follower" (Mark 2:14). But this remarkable initiative of Jesus was exciting news to other Jews who were socially and religiously avoided. They quickly flocked to Jesus—which made Jesus' conduct all the more scandalous to Pharisees and other religious leaders who would not be seen in the company of such people: "While Jesus was reclining to eat in Levi's house, many tax collectors and those known as sinners joined him and his disciples at dinner. The number of those who followed him was large. When the scribes who belonged to the Pharisee party saw that he was eating with tax collectors and offenders against the law, they complained to his disciples, 'Why does he eat with such as these?'" (Mark 2:15-16).

Jesus answered that his mission was precisely to those in deepest need—an initiative of God's grace to the sick and "unjust": "Jesus said to them, 'People who are healthy do not need a doctor; sick people do. I have come to call sinners, not the self-righteous'" (Mark 2:17).

Another great social and religious barrier that Jesus broke through was that between "clean" and "unclean." These terms had little to do with external cleanliness. Certain actions or physical conditions brought about a certain "defilement" or state that disqualified a person from religious and social gatherings until the person was "purified" by a ritual washing after a period of time. Since "uncleanness" was "contagious" and could often be passed on through physical contact with others, it was important that "unclean" people be avoided.

Jesus did not hesitate to welcome and touch such persons. For example, the uncleanness of lepers was regarded as so severe and contagious that they were forced to live together in cemeteries outside the city. They could only speak with others from a distance by shouting while holding a cloth over their faces. They were obliged to warn others of their presence by calling out, "Unclean, unclean!" Jesus however did what no other person of his time would have done. He stretched out his hand, lovingly touched a leper, and cured him: "Suddenly a leper came forward and did him homage, saying to him, 'Sir, if you will to do so, you can cure me.' Jesus stretched out his hand and touched him and said, 'I do will it. Be cured'" (Matt. 8:2-3).

On another occasion, Jesus allowed himself to be touched by a woman who was perpetually "unclean" because of a continual flow of blood for twelve years. What an agonizing existence: not being able to touch others, or allow others to touch her for all these years—never being able to take part in worship or social gatherings. She said to herself, "If I just touch his clothing, I shall get well" (Mark 5:28). These are but brief examples of the countless people who came to Jesus with afflictions that made them "unclean" or "impure."

Again, mental illnesses especially were regarded as caused by the presence of a devil or "unclean spirit" that made the person "unclean." Jesus cured each one by a loving touch or laying on of hands. Mark gives us the example of one such evening when Jesus was surrounded by crowds of sick pressing around him, some shrieking and shouting because of their afflictions: "After sunset, as evening drew on, they brought him all who were ill, and those possessed by demons. Before long the whole town was gathered outside the door. Those whom he cured, who were variously afflicted, were many, and so were the demons he expelled" (Mark 1:32-34).

In regard to women, Jesus' own approach and initiative came as a revolutionary surprise to the people of his time. One factor leading to the isolation of women from men in that culture was that women were affected much more intimately than men by the laws concerning ritual uncleanness. They were unclean for forty days after the time of the birth of a male child, eighty days if the child was a girl (Lev. 12:1-3). Much of women's "uncleanness" had to do with reverence and respect for blood as the source of life. Yet in effect, these regulations placed her in a class apart. At the time of her monthly period, she was "unclean" for seven full days. At the end of this time she had to take a ritual bath. This uncleanness was regarded as so "contagious" that anyone who touched her incurred the same defilement. Not only that, the uncleanness could be incurred by touching her clothing or her furniture or by sitting on the same chair on which she had sat (Lev. 15:19-24).

These restrictions were one factor causing men to be very careful in their dealings with women. Prominent teachers would not speak even to their wives in public. The rabbis of the time did not accept women disciples. In contrast, Luke especially notes that a group of women accompanied Jesus in his travels (8:1-3). Jesus visits the home of two sisters, Martha and Mary. Mary is described in the terms of a disciple, as one "who seated herself at the Lord's feet and listened to his words" (10:39). Jesus takes the initiative in talking with a strange Samaritan woman at a well and even requests that she give him a drink. This is such a surprise to his disciples that the Evangelist John makes this note: "His disciples, returning at this point, were surprised that Jesus was speaking with a woman. No one put a question, however, such as, 'What do you want of him?' or 'Why are you talking with her?'" (4:27).

Another example of Jesus' ideal of imitating the Father is found in his attitude toward the Law, especially the Sabbath regulations. Jesus himself was a faithful Jew and kept the Sabbath as required in the Mosaic Law. At the same time there were areas of possibly conflicting duties. What should be done in these cases, for example, when a sick person needed healing? The answer lies in imitating God himself. He continually does good and heals the sick, every day, whether it is the Sabbath or not. So when Jesus is asked why he heals on the Sabbath he answers, "My Father is at work until now, and I am at work as well" (John 5:17). The rabbis held that even though the Scriptures said that God "rested on the Sabbath," his creative work really continued each day. Jesus appealed to this teaching for justification of his healing work on the Sabbath. He was really doing no more than imitating the Father.

Another way in which Jesus imitated the Father was through watching his Father at work in nature. We already saw some hint of this in Jesus' attitude toward healing or doing good on the Sabbath. He felt obliged to imitate the continual healing creative work of the Father. There is also an important saying that is a central theme of the Sermon on the Mount: "My command to you is: love your enemies, pray for your persecutors. This will prove that you are sons of your heavenly Father, for his sun rises on the bad and the good, he rains on the just and the unjust" (Matt. 5:44-45).

In other words, nature also shows him to be a God of universal love. Initiative and grace make him take the first step even to those who are undeserving. As a result, the disciples are asked to take the same initiative: they are to be ready to greet even strangers on the street (Matt. 5:47); they are actively to do good for, and pray for, their enemies (Matt. 5:43-45). In all this they are to be *perfect* (Matt. 5:48) even as their heavenly Father is perfect. This "perfection" probably has the connotation of maturity; they are to be *mature* sons of God as they imitate the Father's all-embracing love.

For Jesus, nature was a beautiful live mirror of God that continually taught men and women about themselves and about God. The animals and birds were actually teachers who made known God's own universal love and care: "Look at the birds in the sky. They do not sow or reap, they gather nothing into barns; yet your heavenly Father feeds them. Are not you more important than they?" (Matt. 6:26). Even the plants of the field and the flowers taught continual lessons about the loving way that God provides for all: "Learn a lesson from the way the wild flowers grow. They do not work; they do not spin. Yet I assure you, not even Solomon in all his splendor was arrayed like one of these. If God can clothe in such splendor the grass of the field, which blooms today and is thrown on the fire tomorrow, will he not provide much more for you, O weak in faith!" (Matt. 6:28-30).

To sum up: *Jesus' life goal was to bring to completion the hopes of his own, the Jewish people. He felt called to be a true Israelite, a perfect son of God. This meant imitation of God himself through studying his work in nature, and especially in history as found in Scripture. Here he found a God of love and grace who always took the first step to help his people. For Jesus, this meant that his whole approach must be one of loving initiative to the poor, abandoned, and outcasts. Only in this way could the presence of God, through unconditional love, be seen in the world. As a teacher then, Jesus was a person who learned from life itself and expected others to learn in the same manner.*

# 7. Jesus, Teacher and Agent of the Kingdom of God

We can get a better understanding of Jesus the teacher if we compare his approach to that of the leading groups or movements among the Jews of his time. (Judaism was then what we would call "pluralistic" and continued so until the rabbinic consolidation that took place after the fall of Jerusalem. From then on a single type of Judaism, that of the Pharisaic party, dominated almost without challenge until the nineteenth century.)

The first group we will consider is the Zealot party. They were awaiting a chosen leader or Messiah who would be a military leader to help them overthrow the hated Roman rule. Not that they felt they were a real match for the invincible Roman legions; they were confident that God himself would fight on their side to bring them victory. It has been almost commonplace to say, "No, Jesus was certainly not a Zealot; he was a Messiah of peace who wanted to change men's hearts."

This view has been seriously challenged by S. G. F. Brandon.[13] This writer claims that the original picture of Jesus became obscured because the gospels were quite anxious to present him as a Messiah of peace for apologetic reasons: namely, to answer accusations that Christians were followers of a revolutionary leader crucified for sedition under Pontius Pilate. Among his arguments is the fact that one of Jesus' disciples, Simon the Canaanite (which means Zealot in Aramaic), was a member of this party.

It would be very hard to think of Jesus as opposing the central aim of the Zealots, which was to obtain freedom once more for their country, oppressed as it was under Roman rule. A parallel today would be the difficulty of finding an American who does not sympathize with the ideals of the American Revolution. However, the strong emphasis on Jesus' teaching activity in the gospels makes it certain that Jesus believed that military activity could not bring on the kingdom of God. There had to be repentance and change of heart.

Was Jesus a Pharisee? "Surely not," we would answer as we recall the scathing denunciations in the gospels. Yet serious questions need to be asked. As we have noted, the Pharisees were really the cream of first-century Judaism. They were ardent nationalists, anxious to preserve their faith intact in the face of strong pressure to conform to Hellenistic and Roman culture. For them, the Jewish *Torah* was the wall that protected Israel from corruption by pagan influences. Exact and perfect obedience to the law of Moses in all its details was the only road to actuating the kingdom of God. There are a number of indications of Jesus' sympathy with the Pharisees. He often ate in their homes (Luke 7:36; 11:37; 14:1). He defended their authority (Matt. 23:1-3).

At the same time, Jesus' approach showed striking differences from that of the Pharisees. In regard to the *Torah*, the Pharisees held that, in addition to the Pentateuch written Law, an authoritative oral tradition of interpretation had come down through the centuries. Jesus, on the contrary, rejected this approach. He was confident that imitation of the Father, along with an understanding of the essence of the covenant, provided a new basis for interpreting the Law. He felt that his own interpretation, built on this principle, was superior to and even superseded the traditional oral teaching that the Pharisees so zealously guarded.

Another serious point of contrast was Jesus' new approach to ordinary people. The Pharisees looked down on them as "people of the earth" who simply could not keep the many fine points in oral tradition. But Jesus welcomed them and got his best reception from them.

Again, as we have indicated, the prominent rabbis of the time did not seek out their own disciples. A student would search for a well-known Master who might accept him if he were already on the road to being a "perfect observer." However, as we have seen, Jesus did not wait for men to come to him. He took the initiative and chose his own disciples, and chose them from among the kind of people whom the Pharisees would have considered "least likely to succeed." While Jesus *went out* to the sinners, the outcasts, the sick, and the socially and religiously ostracized, the Pharisees carefully avoided them.

Was Jesus an Essene? When the amazing finds of the Dead Sea Scrolls first came to light, exciting journalistic accounts were published about Jesus' relationship to the Essenes[14] — accounts which sometimes "jumped the gun" on serious scholarship. Today we have a much more balanced picture. The points of similarity between the Essenes and Jesus and his community are immediately evident: the close community life, the sharing of a common purse, the importance given to common meals, and the urgent expectation of the kingdom of God are examples. Yet the dissimilarities are even more striking. The Essenes did not "go out" to the world. They only accepted, after careful screening and long probation, those who were already determined to keep the Law perfectly. This is in contrast to Jesus' ideal of going out to men, and his challenge to others to join him in becoming "fishers of men." The Qumran community awaited the building of a new temple where there would be legitimate priests and true sacrifices. Such a hope does not find a place in Jesus' teaching.

The final and most important movement was that of John the Baptist near the river Jordan. It is here that we find an essential key toward understanding what Jesus wanted to do in his earthly life. "When John the Baptizer made his appearance as a preacher in the desert of Judea, this was his theme: 'Reform your lives! The reign of God is at hand'" (Matt. 3:1-2).

Jesus' close connection with the Baptist strikes us immediately. He came to the Jordan River all the way from Galilee to be baptized by him. Jesus' own first disciples were previously disciples of John. It was there, probably, that they had their first contact with Jesus (Acts 1:21-22; John 1:35-37). The evidence for a link between Jesus and the Baptist is all the more credible when we consider that this link was somewhat embarrassing to the early church. Explanatory statements had to be made about it because the disciples of the Baptist were found scattered through the Mediterranean world. For example, Paul found a number of them when he came to Ephesus, and he instructed them, convincing them that they should be baptized in the name of Jesus (Acts 19:1-6).

However, not all of John's disciples became Christians. There are echoes in the gospels of controversy between the two groups. The Baptists must have presented a powerful case. We can imagine their principal arguments: "After all, who baptized whom? Did not Jesus come to the Baptist and humbly submit to baptism? Was it not John who came *first*, not Jesus?" In the gospels we find attempts to answer these questions. Matthew inserts an apologetic statement by John, "I should be baptized by you, yet you come to me?" (3:14). The gospel of John finds it necessary to explain that although Jesus came after John, he was really *before* him (1:30).

In this light, we can surmise that the connection between Jesus and the Baptist may have been much stronger than the gospels tell us. In any case, this connection assures us that an essential key to Jesus' life is to see him as a preacher of repentance in view of the imminent coming of the kingdom of God. Jesus takes over and continues the preaching of John with the same proclamation, "Reform your lives! The kingdom of heaven is at hand" (Matt. 4:17). A better translation would read, "The kingdom of heaven is near." Through most of the Greek translation of the Hebrew Scriptures, this is the meaning of the verb. In the thirty-six passages of the New Testament when the verb is not connected with the kingdom of God, the sense is "coming near," rather than "already arrived." Both John and Jesus were proclaiming that the kingdom of God was not to be expected in the indefinite future. Instead, at the present moment it was on the verge of breaking out.

The simple word "repent" indicates the type of leadership that first John and then Jesus wished to exercise: it shows that repentance and a new direction of life were to be the first concerns. The call to repentance was the familiar call of Jeremiah and Ezekiel, indicating that John and Jesus were preaching in the tradition of the prophets. "Action now" was Jesus' message: "don't just wait for something to happen." Jesus' approach was to begin to carry out the works of the new age at the present moment, rather than to wait for the future. "This is the time of fulfillment" (Mark 1:15). The time to which the prophets looked forward is about to arrive; it is no longer in the distant future. So Jesus set about to fulfill the prophecies of the Messianic Age or "last times." He was confident that all the power of God was with him in this task.

Almost every page of the gospels mentions the kingdom of God.

The establishment of the kingdom was Jesus' great burning concern. The expression "kingdom of the heavens," or its equivalent "kingdom of God," is found over a hundred times in the gospels. (By way of contrast, the word "church" is found only twice.) Despite the frequent use of the term "kingdom," it is hard to deduce a brief concrete definition, because it embraced so wide a range of meaning. It might be better to speak of the kingdom of God as a state of things in which people submit to the rule of God, or obey him. In other words, the kingdom of God is where persons make this world God's world, the kind of world he wants it to be.

The Jews summed this all up with the word *shalom*. It was to be a world of peace and justice according to God's original plan. The phrase "kingdom of God" could be applied to all the relations between man and God that go into making this earth God's own world. The kingdom of God is concerned with right relationships between God and persons as well as those between persons. A wide range of beliefs and expectations existed about this coming kingdom that cannot be neatly catalogued, but the following are some of the more common characteristics of this new world order to be ushered in by God's power:

The future kingdom would complete God's own plan for the world. According to the first chapters of Genesis, God had originally planned to have a single united family of human beings who would live in peace and harmony among themselves and with all of creation. However, sin and selfishness had brought about separation and division. God had chosen Abraham and his descendants as a special people to try to reverse this process. Yet it was quite evident that Israel had not succeeded in its role. The coming kingdom would be a time of restoration, a new creation. First of all, Israel would be renewed and gathered together so that it could be truly God's special instrument in serving the coming kingdom. This would take place under a new leader, a Messiah. In the apocalyptic writings there was a tendency to make him into a kind of super-human figure who would almost drop from the heavens.

Once Israel was restored, then the rest of creation would follow also. The age would be truly one of *shalom*, peace. The national social ethnic boundaries that divided people would be erased. "There does not exist among you Jew or Greek, slave or freeman, male or female" (Gal. 3:28), would be the motto of the new age. All the nations would gather around Israel and form one family that would worship the one God. A favorite picture of the new age, a time when oneness, peace and justice would be achieved for the world, was that given in Isaiah 2:2-4: "In the days to come, the mountain of the Lord's house shall be established as the highest mountain and raised above the hills. All nations shall stream toward it; many peoples shall come and say: 'Come, let us climb the Lord's mountain, to the house of the God of Jacob, that he may instruct us in his ways, and we may walk in his paths.' For from Zion shall go forth instruction and the word of the Lord from Jerusalem. He shall judge between the nations, and impose terms on many peoples. They shall beat their swords into plowshares and their spears into pruning hooks; one nation shall not raise the sword against another, nor shall they train for war again."

This image of oneness was actually a reflection and counterpart of the oneness of God himself. His greatest name was "the One," and his very nature was to create oneness in the human family and in the world. The great daily prayer of the Jewish people, repeated countless millions of times over thousands of years has been: "Hear O Israel! The Lord is our God, the Lord alone!" (Deut. 6:4). The great hope of Israel was that all the world would eventually become one just as God is one: "The Lord shall become king over the whole earth; on that day the Lord shall be the only one, and his name the only one" (Zech. 14:9).

This whole final time was considered the time for judgment and the special intervention of God. All would be set in order. The good would be refined and rewarded; the wicked would experience the full consequences of their misdeeds. The social and economic barriers between rich and poor would finally be erased. The entire world was considered to be held in bondage by evil powers masterminded by Satan. His power would be crushed in a final, severe, hand-to-hand conflict that would usher in the last stages of the kingdom. Many believed that the resurrection of the just would also take place at this time.

In earlier times in Jewish history it was thought that this kingdom of God could come about within world history. This we may call the prophetic view of the kingdom of God. However, at the time of Jesus, many Jews despaired of a fulfillment of the kingdom of God in human history. Things were so bad that they felt that God's world could only be ushered in by a mighty act of God that would probably bring an end to world history as we know it. This we may call the apocalyptic view of the kingdom of God.

Jesus combined and transcended both points of view. His theme, as we have mentioned, was "action now." People could prepare for the kingdom only by fulfilling its conditions here and now. For example, the coming kingdom called for a breaking down of the economic and social barriers between rich and poor. Jesus required this "leveling" of his disciples: as we have indicated, they shared a common purse for their own needs and those of the poor. When a rich young man asked to become a disciple, Jesus asked him to sell what he had and share with the poor (Matt. 19:16-22). The coming kingdom envisioned the gathering together of the outcasts of Israel, the lame, the blind, the sick, the afflicted. Jesus did not wait for them to come but went out and showed how welcome they were. He healed them and restored them to full health in the worshipping community of Israel.

The vision of the last times in Isaiah and the prophets also called for the reunion of the Jewish and Gentile world. Jesus himself had limited contacts with Gentiles. Yet on two occasions—the centurion's servant (Matt. 8:5-13) and the Canaanite woman's daughter (15:21-28)—he did not hesitate to cure non-Jews. In fact, in the case of the Roman centurion, he even offered to go to his home. This did not go along with customs of the time; as we have seen, Jews ordinarily did not enter Gentile homes. (Years later, as recorded in Acts 11:3, Peter was criticized by fellow Jewish Christians because he entered the house of a Gentile and ate with him.) The centurion knew about these Jewish sensitivities, and said to Jesus, "I am not worthy to have you under my roof. Just give an order and my boy will get better" (Matt. 8:8). Both Matthew and Luke (7:1-10) tell this story because they are anxious to show that Jesus was initiating the long expected last times of the world in his present action.

We have already seen that Jesus did not believe that the restoration of women to their proper and equal place in society was to wait until a coming future age. Instead, he welcomed them as companions and disciples in his new community. In addition, he went right to the heart of the cause of women's inferior place in society. He declared that the marriage and divorce regulations of the day were no longer to be in force because they were based on an unjust position of men as superiors and almost "property owners" of women as part of the household (Matt. 19:3-9).

The inauguration of the coming kingdom was to be the time of gathering together the outcasts of Israel: the lame, the blind, the sick, the afflicted. This was to be the direct initiative of God himself according to the prophet Isaiah: "Here is your God, he comes with vindication; with divine recompense he comes to save you. Then will the eyes of the blind be opened, the ears of the deaf be cleared; then will the lame leap like a stag, then the tongue of the dumb will sing" (35:4-6).

Once again, for Jesus, this time is the immediate present, not the distant future. Jesus did not wait for them to come but went out and showed how welcome they were. He healed them and restored them to full health in the worshipping community of Israel. When, for example, he cured the leper, it was not a type of "emergency surgery" but a full restoration in every way to the community: "Then Jesus said to him, 'Go and show yourself to the priest and offer the gift Moses prescribed. That should be the proof they need'" (Matt. 8:4). These gifts were the sacrifices which were part of the ritual of reconsecration that was required before the leper could once more take his part in the social and religious life of the community.

Of all the gifts of God expected in the last days of history, one of the greatest was that of unlimited forgiveness offered to sinners. The prophet Zechariah had predicted, "On that day there shall be open to the house of David and to the inhabitants of Jerusalem, a fountain to purify from sin and uncleanness" (13:1). Ezechiel had stated, "I will sprinkle clean water upon you to cleanse you from all your impurities, and from all your idols I will cleanse you. I will give you a new heart and place a new spirit within you, taking from your bodies your stony hearts and giving you natural hearts" (36:25-27).

Jesus proclaimed in a striking manner that the kingdom of God was coming here and now by taking the initiative (as we have seen) to go right out to the market place and invite tax-collectors and sinners to be his disciples. Moreover, he forgave sins himself, as when he said to the paralytic, "Have courage, son, your sins are forgiven" (Matt. 9:2). Some of the scribes thought this was blasphemy on Jesus' part, for they knew well that this was God's own work reserved for the final age (Matt. 9:3).

Just as so many people do now, it was characteristic of people in Jesus' time to look forward to the future and not to live in the present. On one occasion, the Pharisees asked Jesus when the reign of God would come. Jesus replied, "You cannot tell by careful watching when the reign of God will come. Neither is it a matter of reporting that it is 'here' or 'there.' The reign of God is already in your midst" (Luke 17: 20-21).

Jesus must have repeated that phrase, "the reign of God is already in your midst" again and again. It was hard to convince people to open their eyes to the present moment and perceive all the energy and power of God at work. Jesus told them to be alert and read the signs of the times that pointed to God's action in the present moment: "When you see a cloud rising in the west, you say immediately that rain is coming— and so it does. When the wind blows from the south, you say it is going to be hot—and so it is. You hypocrites! If you can interpret the portents of earth and sky, why can you not interpret the present time?" (Luke 12: 54-56).

To sum up: *Jesus' approach was based on grace which meant taking a first step, an act of loving initiative to those most in need. This was in striking contrast to the approach of other religious leaders of the time. His closest ties were with the Baptist movement. This points to Jesus as a teacher and preacher of moral regeneration in view of the coming kingdom. The nearness of God and the imperative of "action now" characterized his teaching. Those who associated themselves with him as disciples could be expected to adopt the same approach. The conditions of the kingdom were to be fulfilled here and now by actual practice on the part of disciples and not relegated to a dreamy future.*

# 8. "Follow Me!" —
# Teaching through Imitation

The goal of Jesus' ministry that we have just outlined sheds special light on his teaching methods. He thought of himself as a chosen messenger and agent of God to announce repentance in view of the coming kingdom of God (Matt. 4:17). The word *metanoia*, "repentance," was a familiar one to the Jews. It recalled the message of the old-time prophets who called people to renewal by taking the covenant or *Torah* as the model of a whole way of living in obedience to God. Hence Jesus was not a lecturer concerned with theoretics, but a practical teacher totally involved with the urgency of pointing out concrete ways of living out the *Torah* in accord with his own interpretation of it.

Jesus taught people above all by his own life, which he explicitly proposed as a model for imitation. Jesus' favorite command was "Follow me," or "Come after me." These are expressions which convey a very strong sense of imitation in the rabbinic language of discipleship.[15] He called men to come after him and become (like him) fishers of men (Mark 1:17). Levi was called to be a disciple with the words, "Follow me" (Mark 2:14). Jesus' apostles were described as "those who followed him" (Mark 6:1). In general, the words indicate someone who does or is willing to do what Jesus himself does: "If a man wishes to *come after me*, he must deny his very self, take up his cross and *follow* in my steps" (Mark 8:34).

The gospel writers emphatically point out that disciples are people who take Jesus' example seriously and follow it. The evangelists do this by underlining the exact obedience of the disciples: e.g., Jesus calls them with the words, "Follow me," and Mark carefully notes, "And they went off in his company" (1:20). Jesus tells them to go out and preach the good news of the kingdom, and the writer notes, "With that they went off" (6:12).

However, Jesus did not merely point to his whole life in general as a model. He constantly provided concrete opportunities for imitation. For example, when he challenged the rich young man to follow him and sell what he had to share with the poor (Mark 10:17-22), Jesus was really asking him to do what he himself had already done. This is indicated by the words Jesus addressed to him: "Follow me." The expression means, "Do what I have done." Now there is good reason to believe that Jesus was poor not by circumstance but by choice, for he was a "carpenter" by profession (Mark 6:3). This really means much more than the modern word would indicate. A "carpenter" in those days was the local contractor who built homes, bridges, and the "skyscrapers" of those days. It would have been a well-paying profession in comparison with other trades. When Jesus left this work to become a traveling preacher of the kingdom, he took the very real risk inherent in leaving a good source of income. If Jesus asked others to be voluntarily poor, it was only because he himself had chosen to be.[16]

A confirmation of this interpretation may be found in a tradition about Jesus given in 2 Cor. 8:9: "You are well acquainted with the favor shown you by our Lord Jesus Christ: how for your sake, he made himself poor though he was rich, so that you might become rich by his poverty." This verse has generally been interpreted in terms of theological "richness"—that Jesus was "rich" in his divinity but became "poor," that is, human, for our sakes. However, Paul is appealing here for a money collection, and a reference to Jesus' voluntary material poverty would have been a powerful argument for giving generously.

Another example of Jesus' method of teaching concerns the special secret of his inner strength. This was his intimate communion with his Father. In his prayer to God, Jesus addressed him as "Abba" (Mark 14:36). This was an Aramaic word used by little children to speak to their earthly fathers in an intimate, special way. There is no record of its use in prayers to God. The Jews did pray to God as a father; however, when they did so they used the formal Hebrew expression for "father" that is found in Jewish liturgical prayer.

The gospel of John views Jesus' prayer to God as "Abba" or "Father" as so unique and daring that it was regarded as blasphemous by some of his enemies and at the root of the cause for his death: "The reason why the Jews were even more determined to kill him was that he not only was breaking the Sabbath but, worse still, was speaking of God as his own Father, thereby making himself God's equal" (5:18). For Jesus' friends and disciples, however, it was a very special way by which they gradually came to understand this identification and close union of Jesus with God his Father. Thus Thomas' confession addressed to Jesus, "My Lord and my God" (John 20:28), represents the final expression of the deep meaning of "Abba" in Jesus' prayer to the Father.

In Luke's gospel, Jesus' prayer made such an impression on his followers that they asked him, "Lord, teach us to pray, as John taught his disciples" (11:1). In those days, it was customary for great religious leaders like the Baptist to teach and assign to their disciples special religious exercises and practices. Jesus does not do this but rather shares with his apostles his own unique manner of dialogue with God (Luke 11: 2). Luke preserves the address "Father" rather than the "our Father" in Matthew 6:9 to preserve the original nature of the prayer of Jesus. The very word "Abba" became so precious to the early followers of Jesus that they used it again and again. Evidence of this practice is found some thirty years later when Paul writes in Greek to Rome to an audience that is unfamiliar with Aramaic, the language of Jesus. Yet he uses the foreign word "Abba" because it has become so important a word in Christian worship and life: "You did not receive a spirit of slavery leading you back into fear, but a spirit of adoption through which we cry out, 'Abba,' (that is, 'Father'). The Spirit himself gives witness with our spirit that we are children of God" (Rom 8:15-16, cf. also Gal. 4:6-7).

In fact, the tradition about the intensity and frequency of Jesus' prayer made such an impression on Luke that he takes special pains to emphasize it. Jesus is in prayer and communion with God at the time of his baptism (3:21). He spends a whole night in fervent prayer before the decision to choose the Twelve (6:12). The transfiguration of Jesus in divine glory is presented as a result and expression of Jesus' prayer (9:29-36). His prayer in the garden becomes so total and intense that his sweat falls like drops of blood (22:44-45). Yet at times it can be a completely joyous prayer as he "rejoices in the Holy Spirit," thanking God for the success of the mission of the seventy-two disciples (10:21-22).

Because Jesus' prayer to God was a total expression of his entire being, his words, gestures, and appearance made such an impression on those who were with him that they were remembered and imitated. For example, his cure of the deaf man with a speech impediment is reproduced in the rites of baptism. According to Mark's description: " . . . he put his fingers into the man's ears and, spitting, touched his tongue; then he looked up to heaven and emitted a groan. He said to him, *'Ephphatha!'* (that is, 'Be opened!')" (7:33-34).

Most impressive of all, however, was the reverence and deep union with God with which Jesus broke bread. The way he looked up to heaven, pronounced a blessing, and broke the bread is carefully recorded both at the multiplication of loaves and at the Last Supper (Matt. 14:19; 15:36). This was so memorable that the two disciples on their way to Emmaus after the death of Jesus were able to recognize him in the unknown stranger by the unique way in which he broke and blessed the bread (Luke 24:30-31).

At the heart of Jesus' whole life-style is his conviction that love is the core and meaning of life. When asked what was the first or great commandment, Jesus does not hesitate. In the gospel of Mark, he answers the question by quoting the great daily prayer of the Jewish people: "Hear, O Israel! The Lord our God is Lord alone! Therefore you shall love the Lord your God with all your heart, with all your soul, with all your mind, and with all your strength" (Mark 12:29-30; cf. Deut. 6:4-5).

Jesus adds a second commandment as closely connected to this first, "This is the second, 'You shall love your neighbor as yourself'" (Mark 12:31). Matthew draws attention to the similarity between the two by adding the words, "The second is like it" (22:39). Luke sees the two as really one and puts them both together in one statement: "You shall love the Lord your God with all your heart, with all your soul, with all your strength, and with all your mind; and your neighbor as yourself" (10:27). Finally, the gospel of John emphasizes love as *the* commandment of Jesus: "This is my commandment: love one another as I have loved you" (15:12).

We have already seen how Jesus' life-style—love-in-action—was shown in his going out to tax-collectors, sinners, and the outcasts of Israel. However, the gospels especially draw attention to two special qualities of Jesus' love: his love even for enemies and his love for others even to laying down his life for them. Matthew sums up the first quality in Jesus' words in the Sermon on the Mount, "You have heard the commandment, 'You shall love your countryman but hate your enemy.' My command to you is: love your enemies, pray for your persecutors" (5:43-44). This kind of love is so striking and unusual that it will be a manifestation of God himself on earth: "This will prove that you are sons of your heavenly Father, for his sun rises on the bad and the good, he rains on the just and the unjust" (5:45).

Matthew takes care to show that this paradoxical love of enemies is to be shown in our behavior, modeled on Jesus' own, even towards Judas. At the last supper Jesus' heart is filled with sorrow as he reflects that one of those closest to him at table, a companion through the years, Judas, is about to betray him. "In the course of the meal he said, 'I assure you, one of you is about to betray me'" (26:21). This is so shocking to Jesus that he can only say of Judas, "Better for him if he had never been born" (26:24).

Yet despite this deep hurt, Jesus does not dwell on his own feelings but on Judas' desperate need for compassion and love. In doing so, he shows him unusual affection by receiving Judas' kiss and embrace at the very moment when he comes to arrest him (26:48-19). He then addresses him gently to show that he still accepts him despite all that Judas has in mind to do: "Friend, do what you are here for!" (26:50).

The gospel of John goes even farther in illustrating Jesus' unique manner of love. Judas is a person who has been entrusted with an important responsibility in the little community. He holds the community purse and takes care of food purchases as well as distribution of alms to the poor (12:6; 13:29). As in Matthew's account of the Last Supper, Jesus is deeply troubled over what Judas is about to do: "After saying this, Jesus grew deeply troubled. He went on to give this testimony: 'I tell you solemnly, one of you will betray me'" (John 13:21). Despite this, Jesus went on to show Judas a special sign of affection. It was customary in those days, as an extraordinary sign of love, to take a very choice morsel of food, or some dainty, and place it in the mouth of a very dear friend. Jesus did this to Judas (13:26). Judas, however, was not open to this loving initiative on Jesus' part, but closed his heart: "Immediately after, Satan entered his heart" (13:27). Yet Jesus still addressed him in a kindly manner so that he might be free to do as he wished: "Be quick about what you are to do" (13:27). John makes special note that no one at the time understood what was happening. Jesus so carefully shielded Judas that the others thought he was going out to buy provisions or give something to the poor, as was customary during Passover (13:29).

John directly connects this striking manifestation of Jesus' love for Judas with a great intervention of God's power and love in the world: "Now is the Son of Man glorified and God is glorified in him" (13:31). In fact, it is this unique type of unconditional love that is at the basis of imitation of Jesus, for it is his very own. A description of this love follows the betrayal of Judas: "Love one another. Such as my love has been for you, so must your love be for each other" (13:34).

Luke also is deeply impressed by this unusual quality of Jesus' love, and mentions several incidents that bring it out strongly. As Jesus is being nailed to the cross, his concern is more for his murderers than for himself. Instead of cursing them, as many condemned people did, he blesses them with a prayer for forgiveness: "Father, forgive them; they do not know what they are doing" (23:34 acc. to some Greek texts). In his dying moments, he is acutely aware of the suffering criminals at his side. This prompts one of them to ask, "Jesus, remember me when you enter upon your reign." Jesus replied, "I assure you: this day you will be with me in paradise" (23:42-43).

The second extraordinary quality of Jesus' love is his willingness to go to the utmost extreme possible—giving up his own life—in order to prove it. This voluntary offering appears to be directly connected to the non-violent attitude and love of Jesus. He did not *have to be* arrested in Jerusalem at this time. Jesus could have evaded the prearranged sign that Judas had given to the attackers. Yet he made the decision to win others only through love and not power. When the Twelve began to resist forcibly under the leadership of Peter with his drawn sword, Jesus holds them back and orders, "Put back your sword where it belongs.

Those who use the sword are sooner or later destroyed by it. Do you not suppose I can call on my Father to provide at a moment's notice more than twelve legions of angels?" (Matt. 26:52-53). The temptation to use a show of power follows Jesus right to the cross. The bystanders insult him and shout, "Come down off that cross if you are God's Son" (Matt. 27:40). Jesus, however, is willing to die rather than trust in any means to win over others except the divine love within his heart.

Thus Jesus' teaching on non-violent love recorded in the Sermon on the Mount is based on Jesus' own life-style, a way of life that answers evil with good, and injury with love: "What I say to you is: offer no resistance to injury. When a person strikes you on the right cheek, turn and offer him the other. If anyone wants to go to law over your shirt, hand him your coat as well. Should anyone press you into service for one mile, go with him two miles" (Matt. 5:39-41). This is why John in his gospel stresses the degree of love to the extent of death as a unique feature of Jesus' love: "This is my commandment: Love one another as I have loved you. There is no greater love than this: to lay down one's life for one's friends" (15:12-13).

To sum up: *"Follow me" meant literally to accompany Jesus and to imitate him. He asked nothing of his disciples that he did not first do himself. Examples of this are his voluntary poverty which was imitated by the members of his little community and the sharing of Jesus' own inner strength through prayer and communion with God. Above all it was shown through his heroic practice of non-violent love, even for enemies, as far as death. As a teacher, Jesus made his way of love known, not by idealistic statements, but by the visible example of his actions.*

# 9.  Miracles—Magic or Teaching?

To the modern mind, the word "miracle" immediately conveys the concept of an event completely beyond the natural order, something that cannot be accounted for by science. However, the ancient world did not think in terms of two orders: a natural order and one above nature. The biblical view held that every event was the result of God's power. They would not merely say, e.g., "It's raining." They would say, "God is raining (making rain fall) on earth" (e.g., 1 Sam. 12:18; Ps. 147-8). What we would call a "miracle" was therefore considered to be an intervention by God that was simply more unusual or surprising than the "ordinary" ones of each day. These unusual happenings or "miracles" were looked upon as special epiphanies or manifestations of God that exhibited his presence and power in a more extraordinary manner. In this view, the miracles of Jesus were first of all divine epiphanies and only secondarily healings and exorcisms.

When we look to the miracles of Jesus, we find that most of them were in the form of healings of people who came in direct personal contact with him. These can be understood best if we examine them in the context of the world-view of the first century. Jesus said on one occasion, "But if it is by the Spirit of God that I expel demons, then the Reign of God has overtaken you" (Matt. 12:28). The exorcisms or healings of Jesus were an essential part of his ministry. They were a sign of victory over the evil spirits—a sign that testified to the dawn of the final age that was to usher in the kingdom of God.

Even a rapid reading of the gospels is enough to provide an unmistakable picture of Jesus as a powerful exorcist. Shrieking devils seem to be found on almost every page. The first story about Jesus' healing in the gospel of Mark is typical. A devil shouts at him in the synagogue, saying, "Have you come to destroy us?" Jesus rebukes the devil and forces him out of the man with a formula of exorcism. The violent convulsions of the man are meant to indicate to the reader the power of the afflicting spirit (1:23-28). The story is meant to provide an introduction to Jesus' work and must have repeated itself many times as we see from Mark 1:32-34: "After sunset, as evening drew on, they brought him all who were ill and those possessed by demons. Before long, the whole town was gathered outside the door. Those whom he cured were many and so were the demons he expelled."

Everywhere Jesus went, crowds followed him and constantly pushed before him men and women afflicted with every kind of disease, and especially those who were mentally ill. To the average person of Jesus' time, the world was truly a spirit-filled universe. In that non-scientific age, almost every kind of human ailment, especially mental illness, was held to be caused by some disturbing spirit. The Jews considered the whole world under bondage as the result of man's sin. It was indeed a "controlled world." People lived in a state of constant fear since they felt there were so many unknown and possibly hostile presences behind the events of each day. This was true of both Jews and pagans of the time.

Jesus' mission was to liberate people from this bondage. He wanted to break the structures and powers of the old world that held them in fear. In his day there was no better way to indicate his victory over the old structures than by powerful exorcisms and healings. For the Jews, the coming of the kingdom meant a great victory over the hostile spirits. Jesus himself pointed to his exorcisms as a sign of the break-through of the final times.

Yet we would misunderstand Jesus' healing ministry if we thought of it as merely a physical cure or a type of "emergency surgery." The ordinary person of his time believed that every sick person was a sinner. Jesus denied this (John 9:3). But he was convinced that sin affected the whole person and consequently every sinner was, in a sense, sick. To turn away from God and one's neighbor meant a serious disorientation of the whole man that had profound physical effects. For this reason, Jesus required faith of those who came to him for a cure. This faith meant a basic openness to God and to the new opportunities and powers available in the approaching kingdom. Thus forgiveness, assurance of God's acceptance and love played an important part in every cure. This was conveyed by direct contact with Jesus, especially by his gentle touch.

The social implication of a cure required the restoration of a man to his full part in community life, especially worship. In those days, as we have seen, many sicknesses brought with them a ritual disqualification from taking part in public worship. This caused social ostracism as well, since many people carefully avoided such persons out of fear of contracting the same defilement.

Jesus' cure of the leper illustrates the above points (Mark 1:40-45). The humble approach of the sick man to Jesus shows he has the basic attitude of faith or trust in God's power acting in Jesus. Jesus touches him and cures him, but that is not enough. His illness has made him both religiously excommunicated by law and a social outcast, for no one would dare come near him. Jesus sends him to the temple priests so he can be judged as restored, offer the required sacrifices and have the requisite re-anointing with oil. Then he can once again take full part in the religious and social life of the people. Every cure of Jesus was a cure of the whole man—physically, spiritually, and socially.

As we have seen, Jesus' miracles were not intended to be scientific demonstrations but immediate indications of God's presence and power. When Jesus performed them, he did not do so in order to give the impression that they were something he alone could do. He wished his disciples to imitate his ministry of healing. Mark notes that Jesus gave this power to his apostles (6:7), when they went out two-by-two on a missionary preaching tour. The evangelist also carefully notes what they actually did: "They went off and preached the need of repentance. They expelled many demons, anointed the sick with oil, and worked many cures" (6:12-13).

As was said above, the essential quality of Jesus' healings was that they were divine epiphanies,[17] manifestations of God himself in action. To bring out this quality, the gospel authors selected those miracles of Jesus which form a strong, and sometimes almost exact parallel to the miracle epiphanies of God in the Hebrew Scriptures. Traditionally, the greatest of these was the miraculous bread from heaven for the children of Israel in the desert of Sinai. This is described as the special work of

God himself: "Then the Lord said to Moses, 'I will now rain down bread from heaven for you'" (Exod. 16:4). For this reason, Jesus' multiplication of loaves is described in the same terms as God's miraculous provision of manna (Mark 6:34-44; 8:1-10 and parallels). In the same way with the two raisings of dead people through Elijah and Elisha (1 Kings 17:17-24; 2 Kings 4:18-37), and the cure of leprosy (2 Kings 5:1-27)— Jesus performs the same miracles to emphasize his works as divine epiphanies. In fact, Luke describes Jesus' raising of the only son of a widow in terms that are a literary parallel to the resurrection of a widow's only son by Elijah (7:11-17).

Since Jesus' miracles are divine epiphanies, and not a type of personal magic, he is able to share this power with his disciples provided they have the essential disposition: *faith*. This is brought out in detail by Mark on one occasion when Jesus' disciples were attempting a cure while Jesus was away on the mountain of Transfiguration. The disciples were trying to cure a young man with severe epileptic-type seizures. Jesus' disciples were unable to effect a cure. So when Jesus returned, the boy's father approached him, explained the desperate condition of his son and said to Jesus: "If out of the kindness of your heart you can do anything to help us, please do!" (9:22). The reply of the father assumed that all that was needed was a magic word or action on the part of Jesus. Jesus however strongly emphasizes in his reply that it is first of all a question of deep faith: "Jesus said, 'If you can? Everything is possible to a man who trusts!'" (9:23). Later on, when the disciples came to Jesus privately to ask him why they were unable to effect a cure, Jesus answers that the healing ministry, which is a divine epiphany, cannot be carried out except by intensive prayer and faith. He told them, "This kind you can drive out only by prayer" (9:29).

An important reason for the rapid spread of the Christian faith in the first century was the successful work of Christian exorcists who carried on Jesus' healing ministry. In doing so, they felt they were not only imitating Jesus, but acting by the same power as he did. The healing stories recorded by the gospels were models used by the Christian exorcists as they continued this work. In fact, they used the very words and gestures of Jesus, such as *ephphatha* (be thou opened) (Mark 7:34), to show they were acting in his name.

To sum up: *Jesus' miracles effectively taught that God was near in his presence and power. Jesus performed them through personal encounters with persons whose faith he stimulated so they would be ready and open to God's love and power. This meant also a full conversion to God and a complete restoration to community life. Jesus did not consider his teaching approach through miracles as a personal prerogative, but as something that could be shared with his disciples. This was built on the conviction that his miracles were divine epiphanies that would continue to show God's presence in the world. They were thus a form of teaching that could be imitated later by Christian teachers in the early Church.*

# 10. Spontaneous Speech and Teaching through Proverbs

When we read the gospels, the intense reaction of people to Jesus' words immediately strikes us. When Jesus spoke in the synagogue at Capernaum, Mark records that the crowds were "spellbound by his teaching" (1:22). Luke is almost lost in superlatives when he describes the people's response to Jesus' teaching. When he relates the story of Jesus' cure and words of forgiveness to the paralytic, he notes that the people "were all seized with astonishment" (5:26).

The surprise elicited by Jesus illustrates the sharp difference between Jesus' mode of teaching and that which was then customary. Rabbinic teaching[18] in those days depended mainly on careful and constant repetition of the master's words. It was the duty of the pupil to repeat exactly the words of his teacher, the *ipsissima verba*. Repetition was considered so important that Hillel used to say, "The man who repeats his chapter one hundred times is not to be compared with the teacher who repeats it one hundred and one times."[19]

When we listen to Jesus' words, we find there is a unique quality of freshness and creativity about them.[20] He is not a memory expert constantly drilling lessons into his pupils. In his own person he brings the Word of God to his hearers. Jesus' speech is not in the form of lectures or prepared speeches; it is a spontaneous, fresh address to persons in their present concrete situation. As we look through the gospels, we find that much of Jesus' teaching takes place in the familiar surroundings of a home, a small synagogue, a little group in a boat or on the seashore. His teaching comes in response to actual questions put to him by his hearers; he enters into dialogue with them.

This creativity was something that could not be "taught" except by example. It was something contagious that might "rub off" through continual contact with him, and through the realization that the same creative word of God was to be carried by his disciples into the world. So far as we know Jesus wrote no words or compendium of his message. The Good News was to travel from person to person through enthusiastic live communication.

Almost every page of the gospels contains examples of Jesus' spontaneous and vibrant speech. Some examples, however, may serve to highlight this feature of Jesus' teaching. Luke especially likes to point out that the atmosphere of much of Jesus' teaching was a familiar home gathering in the setting of a meal. In fact, Jesus and his hungry disciples seem to have been especially open to dinner invitations. They ate at the homes of Pharisees, as well as in those of tax-collectors and sinners (Luke 7:36; 11:37; 14:1). It was Jesus' alertness and acute sensitivity to these people and situations that was the occasion of important teachings. He is amazed at the contrast between the extraordinary affection of a penitent woman and his host, Simon the Pharisee. She slipped into Simon's home and lovingly kissed and anointed Jesus' feet. Simon, however, had been afraid of being too friendly with Jesus and his disciples; consequently, he had omitted some of the usual signs of welcome: the washing of his feet, and the affectionate embrace for the visitor (7:36-50). On another occasion, Jesus omits the ritual ablutions at a Pharisee's home. On seeing the surprise of his host, Jesus shares his views on the importance of inner cleansing, rather than outward ablutions (11:37-44). At another time, invited by a leading Pharisee, Jesus noticed how the guests were pushing and scrambling for the seats of honor near the host and distinguished guest. He calls this to everyone's attention, and uses the occasion to teach that seats at the banquet of the kingdom of heaven result from God's own grace and invitation and not from human striving (14:1-11). Jesus further observes that his important and distinguished host had invited close friends and wealthy neighbors to the dinner. Jesus comments: "Whenever you give a lunch or dinner, do not invite your friends or brothers or relatives or wealthy neighbors. They might invite you in return and thus repay you. No, when you have a reception, invite beggars and the crippled, the lame and the blind. You should be pleased that they cannot repay you, for you will be repaid in the resurrection of the just" (14:12-14).

For Jesus, every event or encounter was an important learning situation in which God was speaking. Being alert to these opportunities would disclose an unusual and deeper meaning behind what might be the ordinary occurrences of each day. For example, Jesus' family and relatives were quite alarmed about his total involvement in the kingdom of God, and the popular enthusiasm about him. At times, Jesus was so absorbed in his work with people that he did not even have time to eat. "When his family heard of this they came to take charge of him, saying, 'He is out of his mind'" (Mark 3:21). "His mother and his brothers arrived, and as they stood outside they sent word to him to come out" (Mark 3:31). The people in the crowded home relayed the message and expected that Jesus would give priority to the request of his family. But for Jesus the occasion was a deep reminder of the inner nature of the kingdom as centered not in natural families but in the community of those who devote their lives to the kingdom of God. "He said in reply, 'Who are my mother and my brothers?' And gazing around him at those seated in the circle he continued, 'These are my mother and my brothers. Whoever does the will of God is brother and sister and mother to me'" (Mark 3:33-35).

Another feature of Jesus' teaching was his use of the brief, unforgettable saying or proverb. In Jesus' usage the proverb was a short but powerful saying that summed up a great deal of experience and action. Such a saying was very difficult to forget because it neatly expressed what had already been a moving experience for his disciples. For example, as we have already seen, Jesus always took a great deal of loving initiative in regard to "sinners" who, because of their "risky" occupations, such as tax collector and merchant, or their way of life, were looked down upon by careful observers of the Law. So Jesus, after spending hours at a tax collector's office and then at the man's home for food and entertainment, would sum this all up for his disciples in a way they could never forget: "People who are healthy do not need a doctor; sick people do. I have come to call sinners, not the self-righteous" (Mark 2:17).

Such a proverb expresses in a few words a deep unforgettable experience. The apostles had actually walked with Jesus into the tax-collector's office. They had enjoyed a meal and table fellowship with men with whom no pious Jew would associate. The brevity of Jesus' teaching points to its depth and power. The words only re-inforced what had already become part of their life-style through imitation of Jesus and association with him.

The use of a few words to summarize a great deal of experience and meaning is found above all in Jesus' own form of prayer. What is called "the Lord's prayer" or "Our Father" was not meant to be a formula of prayer but a collection of short powerful petitions used by Jesus himself. This is indicated by the fact that the gospels of Mark and John do not contain the Lord's prayer as a whole. They do, however, have the various petitions used by Jesus on different occasions. For example, in Jesus' prayer in the garden, Mark has words equivalent to "Father, thy will be done" (14:36). Evidently they were words that Jesus repeated again and again, for Mark notes (using the Greek imperfect tense) that he *kept saying*, "*Abba* (O Father), you have the power to do all things . . ." (14:36). After a period of prayer, Jesus went to his disciples, found them asleep, and returned once more to prayer. Mark notes: "Going back again he began to pray in the same words" (14:39). The gospel of Matthew has Jesus returning a third time saying the same words as before (26:44).

Thus we see Jesus using what several Eastern traditions call a *mantra*, a brief repeated phrase that evokes a depth of meaning. In John's gospel, we find similar petitions: "Father, glorify your name!" (12:28) and "Guard them from the evil one" (17:15). Short repeated prayers like these seem to have been favorites with Jesus. So, when he responded to the disciples' request that he teach them how to pray (Luke 11:1), Jesus really gave them what had already been a most important and intimate part of his life. They were the prayers he would repeat again and again especially in times of crisis as in the garden before his arrest.

To sum up: *Jesus' mode of teaching elicited great surprise and astonishment from the ordinary people. It did not depend on repetition, as was customary in those days. It was based on a spontaneous, creative response to new people in new situations. In addition, Jesus was not a glib talker. He acted first and then summed up the experience with a short proverb that would be very hard to forget. This took a special form in Jesus' form of prayer which was in effect a* mantra *which he shared with his disciples.*

# 11. Drama from Real Life:
# Teaching through Stories and Parables

The title "drama from real life" was chosen because it well expresses the nature of Jesus' parables. Yet they were drama in a new sense: they were descriptions in story form of Jesus' own life-style and approach. They were a complete expression of Jesus himself so vividly portrayed that a response or decision was demanded from the hearer.

Of course, any novel written by an outstanding author is not completely separable from its creator. Regardless of the amount of fiction in it, the book primarily comes out of the life-experiences of the writer. To say that you do not like the book is really to say, to some extent at least, that you do not like the author—because it is so much a part of him. In this sense, every narration by a real story-teller is an expression of his personality and life-style that invites either acceptance or rejection of the person. This was particularly true of Jesus' stories and parables.

However, in Jesus' case, the connection between stories and life was even closer. In those days, story-telling was much more of an art than it is today, when we depend so much on the written word. The story-teller in ancient times became totally involved in his art. He animated his narration with bodily movement, mimicry, singing, and even dancing. Facial expressions were very important in bringing out the meaning of the story.[21] Even when the Bible text was learned by students, it was done through singing the text itself in imitation of the teacher.[22]

We do not have detailed information on Jesus' art of story-telling, but we have enough references in the gospels to picture him as an exceptionally "live" teacher. For example, at the Last Supper, he stripped off his garments, took a washbowl and began to wash the feet of his disciples to bring out the importance of the humble service that should characterize his disciples. When the apostles were arguing about who was to be greatest in the kingdom, Jesus must have truly shaken them by taking a little child, sitting him in his arms in the middle of his followers, and saying, "Whoever welcomes a child such as this for my sake welcomes me" (Mark 9:37).

Jesus' stories and parables were not just imaginary but were illustrations from real life. They were truly "secular" in that they pointed to typical situations faced by his audience. Yet he used illustrations that portrayed his own approach and insight into people's relations to God and one another. So when the stories were told in such a graphic manner, they were really facing his audience with a decision. The natural reaction was to ask, "Where am I in this story?" or "Should I become a disciple?" Jesus actually does end the parable of the good Samaritan (Luke 10:37) by saying, "Go and do the same." Yet he would not even have to say these words; the story alone would have been enough.

Some of the parables of Jesus resemble what Zen practitioners call a *koan*. This is a short riddle or statement that appears non-rational or nonsensical but is meant to shake a person into seeing things at an entirely new level rather than the way in which human beings ordinarily perceive reality. For example, in the parable of the weeds in the field, when the master finds out that an enemy has sown weeds in the midst of his wheat, the servants ask the natural question "Do you want us to go out and pull them up?" They are surprised by the "irrational" answer of the master, "No, . . . pull up the weeds and you might take the wheat along with them. Let them grow together until harvest" (Matt. 13:29-30). The answer is "irrational" because it goes far deeper than the human "rational" way of looking at people. God's own way is that of infinite compassion, waiting, and forgiveness until the last possible moment.

In the same way, in the parable of the laborers in the vineyard, those who had worked hard all day naturally expect much more than those who had worked only an hour. However, God looks at things quite differently. He looks with compassion: those who have worked only one hour would not be able to provide necessary food for their families with only an hour's wage. So the master, representing God, gives to all a full day's wage (Matt. 20:1-16). Not understanding this attitude, the first workers complain that they are being treated unjustly.

The parables also bring out Jesus' whole approach to life in very specific ways. They can be divided into four groups according to which aspect of Jesus' mission they illustrate. These are: (1) Jesus' inauguration of the kingdom, (2) his grace and forgiveness to sinners, (3) the crisis of the kingdom in the decision each person must make, and (4) the commitment or response of the disciple. In each of these we will see that the parable expresses in capsule form something already part of Jesus' life and actions.

The first group are not really parables but rather pointed similes to call attention to the arrival of the long-expected time of God's final intervention in the world. Examples are the shepherd being sent to care for his wandering, strayed sheep (Matt. 18:12-14), and the fig tree bursting forth with leaves to show that the final summer season has arrived (Mark 13:28). This group illustrates Jesus' powerful conviction that God is near.

The second group of parables announces God's grace and forgiveness shown to sinners. To this group belong the parables of the laborers in the vineyard (Matt. 20:1-16), of the lost sheep, the lost coin, and the prodigal son (Luke chap. 15). Each of these latter represent Jesus in action as he goes out to sinners and surprises them by his initiative in approaching them and accepting them.

The third group of parables announces the urgent opportunities presented by the appearance of the kingdom. Decisions must be made now; they cannot be postponed. For example, in the parable of the talents, the sudden appearance of the master forces an immediate reckoning of the amount that his servants have earned (Matt. 25:14-30). In the story of the ten virgins (Matt. 25:1-13), the five sleepy maids are not ready when the bridegroom appears at a time they did not expect.

The fourth group of parables compels the listener to reckon with the necessity of total commitment if he wishes to become a disciple. A real break with the past must be made along with the beginning of a new life. For example, the illustration of the narrow and broad gate shows that the easy way of the past leads to destruction; the new narrow way means heroic effort (Matt. 7:13-14).

Both these third and fourth groups are based on Jesus' own approach. He considered his work so urgent that he left his own home and asked others to be ready to do so also (Mark 1:14-20). He asked a prospective disciple to sell his possessions and to follow him in a life of voluntary poverty (Mark 10:21).

We should add a word about the significance of Jesus' whole approach through parables. The manner itself is typical of "grace to sinners" which is so much a part of Jesus in action. The form of the parable is really a form of art. An artist is a person who first has a new insight into reality and then has the desire and ability to communicate it to others. When others come to see his art, he does not tell them how or what they should see. This is really up to them. If they are truly open to new ways of perception, then the gift of the artist's message will be imparted to them.

Jesus in his parables was a real artist. He presented new ways of looking at God and the world through scenes from everyday life. Those who had "eyes to see" and "ears to hear" would be able to identify themselves in a parable. They would thus come to a new level of understanding and become disciples of Jesus by choosing the way of life which the parables illustrate.

To sum up: *As a master teacher, Jesus knew how to weave the daily life of his audience into his parables and stories. His parables are really a form of reflection on his own way of approaching both God and man in the kingdom. They were a unique means of shaking people out of old patterns to look at life in a new way. As such, they prompt a person to a decision to take on the life-style that the parable or story proposes.*

# Part III

# The Teacher and Teaching
# in the Early Church

In Part II, then, we have studied the unique characteristics of Jesus as a teacher. Focal here is the "kingdom centered" nature of his teaching, based on a deep conviction that God's loving purpose for the world is to make it a world of justice and peace. Disciples, as a "kingdom oriented" community, are to be a "scale model" of what this kingdom is all about as they try to teach others. Jesus as a teacher is an epiphany of God's presence and love to the world. His disciples are chosen vessels to continue and duplicate this mission. To be able to do so, they are equipped with every power and facility that Jesus himself possessed.

Part III takes us into the early church to see how the teaching ministry of Jesus was practiced in early Christian churches. I say "churches" because the early Christian communities, while considering themselves the one universal church of God, considered each local gathering an embodiment of this church. In our study of early Christian teaching we will first, in chapters 12-20, go through the principal New Testament documents that contain significant material on the teacher (the letters of Paul, the four gospels, the letters of James and John). Then we will put together a composite picture of the teacher drawn from the above sources. In studying the gospels, we will keep in mind that they tell us both about Jesus himself and about the situation in the various churches to which they were addressed, and consequently they contain valuable information about early Christian teachers.

# 12.  Paul, Teacher of Teachers

We begin with Paul the apostle because some of his letters, according to most scholars, are among the earliest Christian documents. Paul himself is our most valuable source of information on "teaching methods" used in the early church.[23] It was his special policy never to go where there was already an established Christian church (Rom. 15:20). Consequently, he himself taught the first Christian converts in each new place. When a church had been established and new converts needed instruction after Paul's departure, the teachers followed the same approach as had Paul.

The first letter to the Thessalonians, written about 49 or 50 A.D., may be the earliest Christian document that we possess. Here Paul definitely states that the first Christians learned their new way of life by imitating the "little church" composed of Paul and his companions. He wrote, "Now, my brothers, we beg and exhort you in the Lord Jesus that, even as you learned from us how to conduct yourselves in a way pleasing to God—which you are indeed doing—so you must learn to make still greater progress" (1 Thess. 4:1). He appealed to their memory of the life-style of the apostolic team: "You know as well as we do what we proved to be like when, while still among you, we acted on your behalf. You in turn became imitators of us and the Lord" (1:5-6).

Not merely general, but also specific modes of imitation are urged in this letter. For example, Paul and his companions worked "day and night" (2:9) in order to win the respect of outsiders. He therefore reminds the Thessalonians likewise to work hard so they will give a good example to those outside the community (4:11-12). Again, personal attention and individual encouragement were characteristic of the apostles: "We exhorted every one of you, as a father with his children, we encouraged you . . . to make your lives worthy of God . . ." (2:11-12). In the same manner, he instructed the converts to "encourage one another, and build up one another" (4:18; 5:11).

The letters to the Corinthians make their strongest arguments through an appeal to Paul's example. In 1 Corinthians he writes, "It was I who begot you in Christ Jesus through my preaching of the gospel. I beg you then, be imitators of me" (4:15-16). Again, "Imitate me as I imitate Christ" (11:1). This verse is of special interest because it shows that imitation of Christ does not mean some abstract example or memory of the past, but an imitation of the life of Christ as exemplified in Paul. Later we will show the implications of this teaching for Paul's concept of apostolic tradition.

Specific examples of this imitation are found throughout this letter. Divisions had sprung up in the community with little groups gathering around their favorite teachers and often judging one another (1 Cor. 1:10-17). However, Paul refuses to judge his fellow teachers; this is God's work (3:5-15). He is one at heart with Apollos, one of the favorite Corinthian teachers. Their unity should be an example for the Corinthians as well: "I have applied this all to myself and Apollos by way of example for your benefit. May you learn from us" (4:6).

In other matters, also, Paul carefully points out his own practice as a model for Christians. The new converts at Corinth preferred the showy, individual ecstatic gifts of the Spirit such as tongues (1 Cor. 12-14). Paul states that he himself possessed this gift (14:18), yet for their benefit he preferred not to use it in public gatherings but to teach and prophesy (14:6,19). In addition, when he states that the celibate life is preferable to marriage in view of the imminence of the kingdom, his own life as a celibate stands behind his words (7:6-7). Again, a great cause of division in the community was the question of eating meats that had at some time been sacrificed to idols but were now sold in the market or in a restaurant. Paul affirms the principle of freedom of conscience, yet states that this freedom should never be the cause of a brother's downfall (8:11-12). In his own life, he would rather never eat meat than cause a brother to fall (8:13).

On reading 2 Corinthians, we can see that Paul was rather reluctant to communicate through letters. He deeply regrets that he was not able to visit the Corinthian Church again as he had planned (1:15). In fact, he does not rely on letters, as others do who put their trust in impressive letters of recommendation. His "letter" is the community itself which he has formed as a living print of its founder: "You are my letter, known and read by all men, written on your hearts. Clearly you are a letter of Christ which I have delivered, a letter written not with ink but by the Spirit of the living God, not on tablets of stone but on tablets of flesh in the heart" (3:2-3). These verses, filled with such deep feeling, tell us to what extent Paul considered the community to be modeled on the lives of the apostles who founded it.

Paul's own criterion for a true apostle is of special interest: it is a manner of life completely dedicated to others even when this entails intense suffering and heroic personal sacrifice. In 2 Corinthians, he writes "In all that we do we strive to present ourselves as ministers of God . . ." (6:4). Among these sufferings are trials, difficulties, distresses, beatings, imprisonments, riots, hard work, sleepless nights, and fastings (6:4-5). These are the actual proofs that he has been sent by Christ; they are the criteria of an apostle. This is the way he teaches people what it means to be a Christian.

This letter contains a specific, very personal reference to imitation. Someone had made a quite serious attack on Paul, which prompted him to write a letter in sorrow and tears (2:2-4). In this letter he had asked the community to take severe action against the offender. Now, however, he writes them to forgive the man just as he himself has forgiven him, despite the severe injury to his reputation: "If you forgive a man anything, so do I. Any forgiving I have done has been for your sakes and before Christ" (2:10).

We find details in 2 Corinthians, chapters 8-10, about Paul's most ambitious and daring project. This was to take up a collection among the Gentile churches to aid the poverty-stricken Jews in the Jerusalem church. Even the word "daring" is completely inadequate to describe the task when we recall the almost insurmountable religious, economic, and social barriers that separated Jew and Gentile at this time.

It is interesting to note that in appealing for this collection, Paul recalls the example of Christ himself, "How for your sake he made himself poor though he was rich, so that you might become rich by his poverty" (2 Cor. 8:9). We have already pointed out that the reference is probably more to actual poverty than to "theological" poverty. So here, once again, we find an appeal to a tradition of Jesus' own way of life. It is also to be noted that Paul does not give lectures on poverty, but actively participates in a real sharing between Jew and Gentile, a sharing which he considers a mark of the true gospel.

Paul's fiery letter to the Galatians has often been called the gospel of Christian freedom. Paul has to defend the gospel of Christ against those who were claiming that the Good News required a person to be also a Jew in the sense of adherence to many of the observances of the Mosaic Law. This would make it practically impossible to gain Gentile converts. It would also make Jew-Gentile fellowship virtually non-existent if the Jewish food regulations were strictly observed. Paul begs the community to follow his example in this matter. He writes, "I beg you, brothers, to become like me, as I became like you" (Gal. 4:12). He illustrates this with the powerful imitation image of the child-parent relationship: "You are my children, and you put me back in labor pains until Christ is formed in you" (4:19).

Once again, Paul's great appeal is to his own example. He above all was a Jew of Jews, a perfect observer of the Law, a fanatic persecutor of the church of God (Gal. 1:13-14). His own conversion was a great act of God's grace, and he has never gone back to the Law despite persecution and great difficulties. He even had to go as far as to rebuke Peter himself for compromising the gospel in order to observe the Law.

This confrontation with Peter took place when Peter visited Antioch. At first he freely ate with Gentile Christians, despite the Jewish dietary laws. However, when other Jews came up to Antioch from Jerusalem, he refused to eat with the Gentiles and only ate with his fellow Jewish Christians. In effect, this was saying in action that the Gentiles were second class citizens who needed something more in order to be perfect Christians. Paul directly withstood him (Gal. 2:11). In front of the whole assembly he called Peter to task for not living the truth of the gospel in practice (2:14).

The letter to the Galatians ends with a powerful thrust at Paul's enemies. They may glory in other marks on their body (circumcision) but he will glory only in the marks, *stigmata*, of the Lord Jesus. These marks are the visible testimony of his sufferings: they are the lash-marks on his body as the direct result of persecution for the truth of the gospel. Thus they identify him with Christ himself who suffered in the same way.

Philippi, Paul's first church in Europe, was his favorite community. They were so faithful to him that they supported him in his work wherever he went, sending letters and gifts, and even giving him personal service when he was in prison. So we would expect the Epistle to the Philippians to be a most intimate letter. Indeed, it is here that he makes his strongest appeal to the manner of life they learned by imitating him when he first taught them. He writes, "Be imitators of me, my brothers. Take as your guide those who follow the example that we set" (Phil. 3:17). He recalls their first learning experience in these words, "Live according to what you have learned and accepted, what you have heard me say and seen me do" (4:9).

Because some discord in the Philippian community had disturbed Paul deeply, he makes a stirring appeal for unity based on the example of Christ himself: "Your attitude must be that of Christ" (2:5). What follows is an ancient Christian hymn which tells how Christ did not seize power and equality with God for himself, but humbled himself in loving personal service for others even as far as death. Therefore God raised him up and gave him as a gift the new name of LORD of heaven and earth (2:5-11). If Christians follow this example, their bodies will likewise be raised in conformity with that of Christ (3:20-21).

We can take this letter to Philippi as an example of a theme common to all Paul's letters—a theme which could easily be taken for granted without recognizing its implications. Paul always asks his converts to pray for him and his work. He feels that prayer is an all-important factor in his work. Since he had instructed these Christians himself, this prayer must have been something they learned from him. In fact, his letters seem like long prayers, so often does he "bless" or thank God and pray for those to whom he is writing. For Paul could not think of his Christians without praying for them, as we see in the opening greeting of Philippians: "I give thanks to my God every time I think of you—which is constantly, in every prayer I utter" (1:3-4).

In regard to prayer, Paul had taught them that through the gift of the Spirit they were able to speak intimately with God as "Abba," Father, with the same confidence as Jesus himself (Gal. 4:6-7). From Paul's letters we can understand that this was already an intimate part of his own life. Over a hundred times he refers to the Father, especially in connection with Jesus. For him, God is the Father of Jesus, and Jesus taught people to pray to God as "Abba." It was through contact with Paul and his company that the first Christians learned to pray in the same manner.

A delightful final touch to the theme of imitation is found in Paul's brief letter to Philemon. The latter was a well-to-do convert of Paul's whose home had become an important church center where Paul had stayed many times. A slave of Philemon had robbed his master, run away, and come to Paul who was then in prison. Paul instructed him and baptized him. The slave stayed for a time near Paul in prison in order to care for his needs. Finally, the Apostle sent him home with a message to his former master asking for forgiveness, acceptance as a brother, and even his freedom.

Of special interest here is the way in which Paul regards the slave once he has instructed him. He is "my child, whom I have begotten in prison" (Phil. v. 10). In sending him back to his master he is really sending back his very heart (v. 12). Hence Philemon should receive him as Paul himself (v. 17). This illustrates the degree to which a disciple was expected to be like his teacher. Since, as a Christian, the runaway slave has now become truly a brother to Paul, the apostle asks his master to receive him no longer as a slave but as a beloved brother. As a brother, Paul agrees to pay back any money the slave owes his master. Paul is confident that Philemon will do even more than he asks (v. 21). This may be hinting that he grant the slave freedom. Throughout the letter, Paul asks nothing of Philemon that he was not willing to do himself.

## PAUL AND APOSTOLIC TRADITION

Paul's insistence on imitation may strike a modern reader as quite egotistical, if he does not understand the apostle's motives. Paul speaks in this way only to churches he himself has founded. As a founder, he has brought to them a living tradition, an *apostolic tradition*[24] that goes back to Jesus himself. His own life has been a necessary mediating link between Jesus and the new churches. Since this point is so important, we will illustrate it with pertinent texts from his letters. Here we must present again some texts we have already studied but must examine now from a new viewpoint.

Paul is not interested in any kind of slavish or mechanical imitation of his own life: in writing to the Thessalonians he stated, "You became imitators of us and *of the Lord*, receiving the word despite great trials . . ." (1 Thess. 1:6). The persecution that Paul undergoes is really that of Jesus himself.

Paul makes a very strong appeal to his *apostolic authority* in 2 Thess. 3:6-7, "We command you, brothers, *in the name of the Lord Jesus Christ*, to avoid any brother who wanders from the straight path and *does not follow the tradition you received from us*. You know *how you ought to imitate us.*" Paul then goes on to describe the manner of his life, in particular his hard work in self-support in order to avoid imposing on anyone. He did this for them as an *"example to imitate"* (2 Thess. 3:9). The solemn injunction *in the name of the Lord Jesus Christ* shows the authority behind his statement. Yet it is not an authority based on the power of dominion, but a power based on a life that is led in conformity with the gospel. Paul has been the founder of the community. Thus he has come to them as Christ himself. As a consequence, since his own life is the direct link with Christ, he can present himself as a concrete example of Christian tradition that is to be handed on to others. *This is his apostolic authority.*

We find the same pattern of thinking in Philippians, but brought out indirectly. As we have pointed out, Paul exhorts them to "have this in mind in you which was also in Christ Jesus" (2:5). Once he has presented Christ as the supreme model, then he can say, "Be imitators of me" and "take as your guide those who follow the example that we set" (3:17).

In 1 Corinthians, Paul faces opponents who make a claim to apostolic authority through letters of recommendation or association with prominent church leaders in Judea. He counters this by presenting the criteria for a true apostle. When he writes "apostle," it is in the literal sense of one sent by Christ to act on his behalf. An "apostle" is a traveling founder of new churches who has gone through the same experience of hardship and suffering as Jesus himself. Paul wants to be regarded as a "servant of Christ" and "administrator of the mysteries of God" (4:1). Then he points out how his claim to this regard can be verified: "Up to this very hour we go hungry and thirsty, poorly clad, roughly treated, wandering about homeless. We work hard at manual labor" (4:11-12).

It is only because he has fulfilled these criteria and has been their father through the preaching of the gospel (4:15) that he can say, "Be imitators of me" (4:16). At this time Paul cannot actually be present to furnish them that example, so he sends Timothy as a "beloved and faithful son" to remind them of his "ways in Christ" (4:17). When Paul asks for imitation it is only that they follow him in his own imitation of Christ: "Imitate me, as I imitate Christ" (11:1).

Paul does not use such imitation formulas in writing churches that he himself has not founded. Instead, he uses general terms that refer to acting as Christ did (Rom. 15:7; Col. 3:14). In view of this fact and the texts cited above, we can state with a high degree of certainty that Paul's exhortations to imitate him are based on the fact that a community has accepted the gospel of Christ from him. This gospel, as preached by him and lived by him, constitutes his own personal witness to Christ. Paul represents him and acts in his name by carrying on the same role and mission as a servant of God. His "apostolic authority" is the authentic embodiment of the gospel in his own life to such a degree that it can constitute a living Christian tradition to be handed on to others.

## Paul, Living Example of Jesus' Teachings in the Sermon on the Mount

For Paul, there was no doubt at all that Jesus' teaching was centered in love. Thus he could summarize the life-style of Jesus in one word: love. He calls the Christian life-style "the rule of love" (Rom. 14:15). This is brought out in detail when he writes to the Galatians: "The whole law has found its fulfillment in this one saying: 'You shall love your neighbor as yourself'" (5:14). He also calls it the "Law of Christ" (6:2). He expresses this in a similar form in the letter to the Romans: "Owe no debt to anyone except the debt that binds us to love one another. He who loves his neighbor has fulfilled the law. The commandments, 'You shall not commit adultery; you shall not murder; you shall not steal; you shall not covet,' and any other commandment there may be are all summed up in this, 'You shall love your neighbor as yourself.' Love never wrongs the neighbor, hence love is the fulfillment of the law" (13:8-10).

Yet Paul is not content to use the word "love." It must be exemplified in his own life in the same way as it was in the life of Jesus. It is something taught by example rather than taught by words. Paul has made his own the deep personal insight of Jesus that loving others, even enemies, means loving as God does. Like Jesus, Paul responded to injuries, persecution, and even hatred with a beautiful non-violent love, the kind of love which continually surprises and amazes the world. In his own experience as an apostle, Paul was often insulted, slandered, put in prison, and even tortured. Yet he could write, "When we are insulted, we respond with a blessing" (1 Cor. 4:12). Paul was particularly struck by Jesus' love even for those who betrayed him. When writing about the Lord's supper and trying to convey its inner meaning as a feast of sharing and love, Paul takes special note that it took place "on the night in which he was betrayed" (1 Cor. 11:23).

An important aspect of Paul's life-style as a teacher was this unique quality of love, similar to that of Jesus. Many of his own Jewish brothers bitterly opposed him because they could not accept his stand on receiving Gentile converts without the obligation of the biblical laws about circumcision and other traditional observances. It is with sadness that he writes, "Five times at the hands of the Jews I received forty lashes less one" (2 Cor. 11:24). He had also to suffer from the "false brothers," fellow Christians who tried to undermine all his work and efforts (2 Cor. 11:26). Yet these experiences did not make him bitter. They only made him draw deeply on the Spirit within, the source of loving forgiveness. When Paul wrote to his communities about love, he could speak from personal experience. "Bless your persecutors; bless and do not curse them" (Rom. 12:14). "Be kind to one another, compassionate, and mutually forgiving, just as God has forgiven you in Christ" (Eph. 4:32).

As we have already seen, an outstanding characteristic of Jesus himself was his special love and interest in the poor, the outcasts, the sick, the weak, and the lowly. Paul was especially moved by this quality of Jesus' love. Whenever possible in his letters, he shows that consideration for the weak is a sure test of love's sincerity. For example, as we have seen, some wavering Christians in Corinth and Rome did not feel they could eat meats that had been previously offered in sacrifice to idols. Paul writes, "Extend a kind welcome to those who are weak in faith" (Rom. 14:1). He sees this as a real imitation of Jesus himself, who tried to build up others—especially the weak: "We who are strong in faith should be patient with the scruples of those whose faith is weak; we must not be selfish. Each should please his neighbor so as to do him good by building up his spirit. Thus, in accord with Scripture, Christ did not please himself" (Rom. 15:1-3). In his own life-style, Paul himself showed an active sympathy for the weak: "To the weak I became a weak person with a view to winning the weak" (1 Cor. 9:22).

Many other indications that Paul knew and practiced Jesus' teachings on love as found in the Sermon on the Mount might be cited. For example, Jesus had emphasized the non-judgmental nature of love when he declared, "If you want to avoid judgment, stop passing judgment" (Matt. 7:1). Paul gives special attention to this quality of love. In writing to the Galatians, he emphasizes that they should try to help sinners by gentle and helpful advice, carefully avoiding comparisons or judgment: "My brothers, if someone is detected in sin, you who live by the spirit should gently set him right, each of you trying to avoid falling into temptation himself. Help carry one another's burdens; in that way you will fulfill the law of Christ. If anyone thinks he amounts to something, when in fact he is nothing, he is only deceiving himself" (6:1-3).

In reference to the Christians who were divided on the question of eating foods sacrificed to idols, Paul confronts both groups by writing, "Every one of us will have to give an account of himself before God. Therefore we must no longer pass judgment on one another" (Rom. 14:12-13).

Again, Jesus had taught by word and example that the ordinary laws of justice and retribution are not sufficient. A new law of love was necessary, a love that responds to injuries, even lawsuits, by acts of generosity. "But what I say to you is: offer no resistance to injury. When a person strikes you on the right cheek, turn and offer him the other. If anyone wants to go to law over your shirt, hand him your coat as well" (Matt. 5:39-40).

Paul sees this teaching as applicable in his own life and that of the community. He was quite shocked to learn that the Corinthians were going to ordinary civil courts to settle their disputes. He asks why they cannot come to agreement and reconciliation by solving the matter within the community: "Must brother drag brother into court, and before unbelievers at that?" (1 Cor. 6:6). Then he asks why they do not willingly accept injury and win over others through love, rather than through retribution: "Why the very fact that you have lawsuits against one another is disastrous for you. Why not put up with injustice, and let yourselves be cheated?" (1 Cor. 6:7).

To sum up: *Paul's witness is especially valuable in our assessment of early Christian teaching since he was a founder of new churches and set a pattern which others followed. Throughout his letters, he continually refers to his readers' vivid memory of his own life-style. It was this life in Christ that was to be their guide. Yet Paul is not interested in any mechanical imitation of himself. He is interested in* apostolic tradition, *meaning the imitation of Christ himself as mirrored in the apostle's own personal response to the gospel, since Paul has been the first living link between his converts and Christ.*

# 13. Mark and Christian Teachers of the Way of the Cross

The essential key to understanding the special characteristics of Mark's gospel is found in chapter 13. There we find the only definite clues to the historical situation of the church to which this gospel is addressed. Jesus' apocalyptic discourse in this chapter appears as a climax to his life: It represents his last words and testament before the opening of the passion account in chapter 14. The historical references are to the destruction of Jerusalem (13:2), to be accompanied by a profanation of the Temple (13:14). Here the writer is not simply narrating either past or future history, he is writing a message relevant to the audience to which the gospel is directed. This is why the liturgical reader of the message is asked to make special note of the present implications of the words he announces to the assembly (13:14).

We may assume, then, that the events of the Jewish war with Rome, 66-70 A.D. must have had profound effects both on Mark and his audience. Jerusalem was the capital of the Jewish world. The catastrophic event of its present, past, or future destruction would be a central, decisive world event—an extraordinary intervention of God signaling the beginning of the last days of the world. Among Christians it would have prompted an intense expectation of the imminent return of Jesus in glory.

As a result, many Christians were looking for signs of this powerful coming. Some were claiming that Christ was already present within them and working in power: "Any number will come attempting to impersonate me. 'I am he'" (Mark 13:6). As a proof, they pointed to the miraculous signs and wonders they were able to produce (13:22). Mark refers to them as "false Messiahs and false prophets" (13:22).

Against such tendencies, the author directs a two-pronged attack throughout his gospel: (1) He argues that Christian hope for the future is really disassociated from the destruction of Jerusalem. To prove his point, he deliberately "de-Judaizes" Jesus in his gospel and gradually separates him from the stream of Jewish expectations about the Temple, the Law, and the future. As a consequence, the destruction of Jerusalem is not the end-point of time: a period of history is to follow that will end in a worldwide manifestation of the return of Jesus that is independent of the fate of Jerusalem (Mark 13:24 ff.); (2) He vehemently disagrees with the "triumphal" Christology of his opponents. Instead he presents an alternate picture of a suffering, crucified Messiah[25] recognized as Son of God by those who follow him along the same path. He is writing for a community under persecution, needing a truly human model and example as they face the possibility of suffering and even death for their faith.

In the gospel of Mark, the only explicit reference to teaching on the part of anyone but Jesus is in 6:30. Here the Twelve, after their preaching tour, return to Jesus and tell him all they had done and *taught*. This teaching concerns the need for repentance in view of the coming kingdom (6:12). In reading through the gospels it is hard to distinguish what belongs to the original historical situation and what belongs to the later life of the church. Since the church considered Jesus the teacher as a model, the descriptions of Jesus tell us much about the activity of later Christian teachers. The missionary journey of the Twelve probably reflects to a large extent the preaching experience of the later church, which contained an urgent appeal for repentance (cf. Acts 2:38) and thus duplicated and continued Jesus' own essential preaching on repentance.

On closer examination, however, there appears to be much more explicit indication that Mark considers the Twelve as successors to Jesus insofar as they carry on his mission of teaching, preaching, and healing. The literary parallel is probably the last blessing and testament of Jacob (Israel)—where he transfers to his twelve sons his own powers and entrusts to them the mission that God has given him (Exod. 49). This parallel is highly developed in Matthew, but the essential elements are already in Mark. The mission of the Twelve is placed in the context of forebodings about the death of Jesus. He has just been rejected at Nazareth, his own home town (Mark 6:1-6), and news reaches him about the death of the Baptist, his forerunner in teaching repentance (6:14-29). Then the Twelve are described as doing what Jesus did: preaching repentance (6:12), expelling demons, and curing the sick (6:13).

Some examples of Jesus' teaching point especially to the work of early Christian teachers as his successors. Jesus' teaching concerning the Scriptures' fulfillment in his death and resurrection probably belong to this area. We are led to think in this direction by a number of hints in the gospels that the understanding of Jesus' death and resurrection in terms of the Hebrew Scriptures was something that took place after his death through the work of the Holy Spirit.

For example, in Luke's gospel it is specifically the Risen Christ who enlightens the disciples in regard to the meaning of the Scriptures as they journey toward Emmaus. He tells them, "Did not the Messiah have to undergo all this so as to enter into his glory?" The writer then adds, "Beginning, then, with Moses and all the prophets, he interpreted for them every passage of Scripture which referred to him" (24:26-27). Likewise the gospel of John tells us that Peter and John did not know about the scriptural teaching on Jesus' resurrection until some time after his death. When the two apostles come to the empty tomb, the writer notes, "Remember, as yet they did not understand the Scripture that Jesus had to rise from the dead" (20:9).

Consequently, if we wish to examine a central teaching area of the early church, we must examine the sections in Mark where Jesus speaks of his coming death and resurrection, especially 8:31 ff., 9:31 ff., and 10:32 ff. Each of these passages is followed by a collection of teachings on discipleship, showing how a disciple can follow Jesus along the same way of heroic suffering even to death. Mark seems to give special emphasis to this theme in view of the need—in the church he is addressing—for Christian teaching on the cross.

The following is a schema of these three teaching sections in Mark along with a brief summary of the content:

## TEACHINGS ON DISCIPLESHIP

| Gospel of Mark | Summary of Passage |
|---|---|
| 8:31 | The First Prediction of Jesus' Death and Resurrection |
| 8:32-33 | Jesus calls Peter "satan" because he looked for a way other than that of the cross. |
| 8:34-38 | Every Christian must be ready to take up his cross like Jesus. "Deny yourself, take up your cross, and follow me" is the only motto for a follower of Jesus. |
| 9:1-13 | The transfiguration—divine glory shining through Jesus assures that suffering discipleship leads to glory. Jesus' sayings about the cross are so essential, yet seemingly impossible, that a voice from heaven commands the disciples to hear Jesus as God's son. |
| 9:14-29 | The healing of the epileptic. The way of Jesus calls for extraordinary faith in face of the humanly impossible: "Everything is possible to a man who trusts." The disciples must have this intense faith to continue the healing mission of Jesus. |
| 9:30-32 | The Second Prediction of Jesus' Death and Resurrection |
| 9:33-35 | The cross of Jesus reverses all human values. The disciple who is greatest will be least and servant of all because he will be most like Jesus. |
| 9:36-42 | The power of identification with Jesus and acting in his name. |
| 9:36-37 | Children are especially more precious in view of their union with Christ. |
| 9:38-40 | Exorcisms can be performed by anyone if done through Jesus' name and faith in him. |
| 9:41 | To receive a disciple, even with a cup of cold water, is to receive Christ himself. |
| 9:42-49 | Scandal is to be avoided at great cost since the gift of faith is so precious. |
| 9:50 | The disciples have the responsibility to influence the world. |
| 10:1-31 | Jesus' "Impossible" Sayings. |
| 10:2-12 | On marriage and divorce. The union between man and woman in marriage is not to be governed by property relationships. It is a personal covenant coming from God himself. |
| 10:13-16 | One should accept the reign of God with the innocence and total belief of a child. |
| 10:17-31 | On riches and voluntary poverty for disciples of Jesus. "Go and sell what you have and give to the poor" is a hard saying that few will listen to. Jesus repeats twice: "How hard it is for the rich to enter the kingdom of God!" Yet, he stresses "for man it is impossible but not for God. With God all things are possible." |
| 10:32-34 | The Third Prediction of Jesus' Death and Resurrection |
| 10:35-40 | James and John. The places in the future kingdom of God are not pure gift. The cost of discipleship is immense. There is a necessity to be "baptized" into Jesus' death. |
| 10:41-45 | The greatest in the kingdom are the least of all: those willing even to sacrifice their lives—like Jesus who has come not to be served but to serve. |
| 10:46-52 | The blind beggar Bartimaeus is the figure of all those whose eyes must be opened in faith before they can follow Jesus on the way to Jerusalem and the cross. |

This triple section on discipleship reminds us of the early baptismal catechesis in which the description of the new Christian "Way" is developed out of the meaning of the death and resurrection of Jesus, as well as in association with it. We saw how, in Romans, chapter 6, the convert symbolically joined himself to Christ by stepping into the waters and then rising up again after his baptism to begin a new way of life. This rite follows the line of the three summaries on discipleship in Mark.

There are strong baptismal hints throughout these three sections. Special emphasis is given to following Jesus (8:34; 10:21) and the Way. James and John are prototypes of those who wish to be joined to Jesus in his kingdom: they must be *baptized* with the baptism with which he is to be baptized (10:35-40). It is in this part of the gospel that we find the largest collection of Jesus' teachings on practical matters of life: marriage, divorce, children, riches. All of this looks very much like the teaching of the Way that characterized baptismal catechesis.

To sum up: *The gospel of Mark presents the Twelve as models for the teacher in the early church who carries on the teaching, healing, and preaching mission of Jesus. This teaching is centered in the cross and indicates a very practical orientation of Christian teachers who point out a new way of life to their converts. The living example of the teacher is meant to be in sharp contrast to some "superstar" Christians who modeled themselves on the image of the divine wonderworker which was so popular in the Hellenistic world.*

# 14. Matthew, Manual for Teachers

The powerful impact of the last verses of Matthew leaves no doubt that his principal concern is to present Jesus as a model for teachers who are to go out all over the world and form new converts in the Christian Way. In his account, Jesus appears to the Eleven on a mountain after his resurrection. He is now enthroned with full power and authority. He then gives them the commission to go out to teach in his name. He will be with them as they do so. The Eleven are to form disciples according to the commandments and teaching of Jesus: "Full authority has been given to me both in heaven and on earth; go, therefore, and make disciples of all the nations. Baptize them in the name 'of the Father, and of the Son, and of the Holy Spirit.' Teach them to carry out everything I have commanded you. And know that I am with you always, until the end of the world" (28:18-20).

Since the Eleven are to carry on the teaching work of Jesus himself, what this gospel tells us about Jesus as a teacher is especially relevant to the teacher in the church to which Matthew's gospel is addressed. First of all, the structure of the whole gospel places special emphasis on Jesus' teachings. The five principal discourses in Matthew are composed of collections of Jesus' sayings and occupy a central place in his gospel. These are the Sermon on the Mount (chapters 5-7); the missionary instructions (chapter 10); the collection of parables (chapter 13); the discourse on the church (chapter 18); and the instruction on the last things (chapters 24-25). Each of these collections is identified by a special introduction and conclusion.

To strengthen his portrayal of Jesus as teacher, Matthew carefully revises the tradition of the miracles that he has before him.[26] He abbreviates the details of the stories in order to heighten the person of Jesus and his words. To a large extent, the miracles become an encounter with the person of Jesus. To make this more effective, the dialogues between Jesus and the persons concerned are strengthened.

As an example, we can look at the cure of the paralytic in Matt. 9:1-8 as compared to the parallels in Mark 2:3-12 and Luke 5:18-26. Matthew's account is one-third shorter than Mark or Luke. The evangelist omits all the descriptive details about the miracle: the description of the place, the house, the crowds, the lowering of the paralytic by four men through the roof. Matthew wants to highlight the person and words of Jesus the teacher and the continuity of his work in the church. For this reason he ends the account with the words (proper to his gospel): "They praised God for giving such *authority* to men" (9:8). Because other details have been omitted, this statement stands out as a follow-up to Jesus' own words, "the Son of Man has *authority* on earth to forgive sins" (9:6). Jesus' own authority as Son of Man is now present in the church, and those who believe experience that same forgiveness of sins through his Risen Presence.

When Matthew "retells" the miracle stories found in his tradition, he is more interested in the message they convey about Jesus himself than in the miracles. He emphasizes three themes:[27] (1) the importance of the person of Jesus, (2) the nature of faith in Jesus, (3) the meaning of discipleship. Thus Jesus is effectively presented more as the powerful teacher than as the wonderworker.

The first theme has already been seen in the story of the paralytic. The second is brought out in the presentation of the miracles as personal encounters with Jesus, omitting all other "unnecessary" details. It is also developed by a more frequent use of the word "faith"—eight times as compared to Mark's five. The third theme is emphasized by a careful retelling of the miracles so that they reflect a continuing situation in the church. For example, in Matthew's description of the stilling of the storm, in place of Mark's detailed setting, Matthew simply writes, "He got into the boat and his disciples *followed* him" (8:23; cf. Mark 8:35-36). In both Matthew and Luke (8:22-25) the frightened disciples awaken Jesus and cry out that they are perishing. In Matthew, this becomes a prayer, "Lord, save us! We are lost!" (8:25). In this way it becomes the continuing prayer of disciples of Jesus in any time of crisis in the history of the church, when they can cry out, "Lord, save us."

Like Mark, Matthew is especially concerned to present Jesus as a man who spoke with *authority*: "He taught with authority and not like their scribes" (Matt. 7:29). However, Matthew is careful to point out that this *authority* is now present in Jesus' disciples and their teaching after the resurrection. Thus, in his missionary discourse (chapter 10), Matthew notes that Jesus gave his disciples the power to preach. He seems to have deliberately omitted a reference to *teaching*. We say this because Mark, his source, had noted that the disciples reported to Jesus what they had done and *taught* (Mark 6:30). Matthew's reason may be this: he wants to show that only after the resurrection will the disciples be able to *teach*, in the sense of forming disciples, for only the Risen Christ will be able to give them the authority and power to do so by his continued presence. Thus it is really Jesus himself who remains behind the teaching work of the church. It may be for this reason that only Matthew records the saying of Jesus that no one is to be called "Teacher" in the church; this belongs to the Christ alone (Matt. 23:8).

Indeed, one of Matthew's main purposes is to establish a direct line of authoritative authentic teaching and power from God, through Jesus, through the Twelve, to teachers in the church. In the ancient world, as was pointed out earlier, authoritative teaching was demonstrated and proved by showing a succession of teachers. This has been well-illustrated by C. Talbert.[28] Greek philosophers made use of this method to trace their teaching back not only to their immediate masters but to those before them. In Jewish circles, the same was true. In the *Pîrke Aboth*, for example, the rabbis give a long list of authentic teachers reaching back for centuries, even to Moses himself. Christians also made use of this motif. The pastoral letters try to show that a true deposit of faith was handed down from Jesus, and then through Timothy and Titus. In the article of Talbert cited above, the author tries to show that a principal purpose of Luke-Acts is to establish a line of succession of authentic teaching from Jesus, to the Twelve, and to the church, in order to combat gnostic tendencies among some Christians. The gospel of John likewise is especially concerned to develop criteria for authentic teaching through use of the succession motif. We will trace this motif for Luke and John in the next two chapters.

In Matthew, the succession theme is developed in 9:35-11:1: the instruction to the Twelve. By way of setting and introduction, Matthew describes Jesus as having completed a tour of the towns and villages while performing three essential tasks: *didaskōn* (teaching), *kērussōn* (preaching), and *therapeuōn* (healing) (9:35). However, he has reached the point where he can no longer continue alone. It is the end time, the harvest, and other workers are needed. He says to his disciples, "The harvest is good but laborers are scarce. Beg the harvest master to send out laborers to gather his harvest" (9:37-38). In addition, Jesus' death is near. Consequently, Jesus hands over to his disciples each of the three powers: to cure (10:1), to preach (10:7), and to teach (28:20). This last, as we have seen, is reserved for the final commission of the Risen Christ.

The strongest indications of a teacher-succession theme come from the clear parallel between the last testament succession story of Jacob (Israel) and his twelve sons and the transfer of powers to the apostles in Matthew. The general lines of parallel are the following: at the end of Jacob's life, a new era is to begin; he must hand over his mission and powers to his sons. The same is true of Jesus. The harvest or end period is at hand; his death is near; the new era, that of the church, is about to begin. Jesus must hand over his work to the Twelve.

The special care that Matthew has taken to describe Jesus' conferring his powers on the Twelve shows that the mission of the Twelve and the transfer of authentic teaching has a central place in his gospel. In the birth story of Jesus, Matthew has indicated that Jesus will carry the divine name, Emmanuel, meaning "God is with us." In the Sermon on the Mount (chapters 5-7), he has shown that Jesus' teaching even surpasses that of Moses, who spoke for God. It carries authority (*exousia*) (7:29). It surpasses that of the scribes who have succeeded Moses as teacher (23:2). Thus it is indeed the teaching of God himself. The miracles of Jesus are divine epiphanies paralleling and even surpassing the greatest miracles of the Old Testament.

Jesus, however, as we have indicated, is approaching the time of his own death, and the end time of the harvest is drawing near. The divine *presence* and *power* within him must be *handed over to* and *shared with* the Twelve. Within this group, he has already singled out Peter as *protos* (Matt. 10:2). Matthew develops this further in special Petrine material about Peter's confession of Jesus as Son of God, along with Jesus' promise that he would be the rock upon which the church would be built. These and other passages (14:28-31; 16:13-20; 17:24-27) indicate the special importance of Peter among the Twelve in the gospel of Matthew.

For Matthew, then, this authority of teaching belongs especially to the Twelve and above all to Peter. In Matthew, no miracles are worked except by Jesus and the Twelve. He omits the story in Mark that others were casting out devils in the name of Jesus and were not forbidden to do so (Mark 9:38-40). At the mountain of Jesus' enthronement and ascension it is the *Eleven* alone who are given the *authority* to teach (Matt. 28:16-20). Peter is the spokesman for the Twelve. He is singled out as the recipient of the keys of the kingdom of heaven, with the powers to bind and to loose (Matt. 16:17-20).

We can better understand this emphasis on Peter and the Twelve in view of the historical situation in which this gospel was written. It was composed at a time when the church was beginning to make an institutional separation from Judaism. If the gospel was written late in the first century, as is generally agreed, then Jesus' original hearers had already died. Therefore it was necessary to establish firmly the tradition about Jesus, especially to counter some over-enthusiastic groups who relied more on charismatic experience than on moral performance (7:21-23).

The position and power of church leaders were stressed by Matthew since they were the necessary agents to combat these movements. These leaders would be "Peter and the Twelve"[29] in the new situation of the church. Yet their position was not to *control* the faithful or the tradition about Jesus. They were faithfully to transmit this tradition and guard it. The Risen Jesus orders them to command obedience to *himself*: "Teach them to carry out everything I have commanded you" (28:20). Matthew is concerned above all about the handing on of this tradition. The task has been entrusted by Jesus to the Twelve, and through the Twelve (now represented by church leaders and teachers) to the church, or "assembly" of disciples.

"The church," however, is not the passive recipient of the work of the Twelve and other teachers. Peter's power of "binding and loosing" (Matt. 16:19) is next present in the *ekklesia* or church. Jesus' word is addressed to the church as he says, "I assure you, whatever you declare bound on earth shall be held bound in heaven, and whatever you declare loosed on earth shall be held loosed in heaven" (18:18). This church also has the divine presence through Jesus wherever disciples are gathered together in his name: "Where two or three are gathered in my name, there I am in their midst" (18:20).

The teaching work of the church leaders was directed to many groups both in the church and outside of it. However, there is an important indication that Matthew was especially concerned about Gentile converts and their baptismal instruction. In the final words of Jesus, the Eleven are to make disciples of the whole *world*, and *baptize* them, while teaching them to observe Jesus' commandments (28:19-20). It would be here especially that teachers would have to show converts what a new way of life in Jesus would mean in their daily lives.

With these practical instructional needs in view, we can see why Matthew takes unusual care to recall those words of Jesus that heighten the importance of example on the part of the disciple who teaches others. It is this example that will draw men to the true faith: "In the same way, your light must shine before men so that they may see your acts and give praise to your heavenly Father" (5:16).

For this reason, he paints a vivid picture of the disaster that takes place when a disciple does not follow the true way and then teaches others: "Whoever breaks the least significant of these commands and teaches others to do so shall be called least in the kingdom of God" (Matt. 5:19). The ideal is to *do* and to *teach*: "Whoever fulfills and teaches these commands shall be great in the kingdom of God" (5:19).

For Matthew, example was the highest form of teaching. He illustrates this by the saying of Jesus, "No pupil outranks his teacher, no slave his master. The pupil should be glad to become like his teacher, the slave like his master" (10:24-25).

To make the point of *doing* and *teaching* as forcible as possible, Matthew uses the verb "do" some twenty times in the Sermon on the Mount. The discourse closes with a powerful image to express the need of uniting together both *hearing* and *doing*: Everyone who hears Jesus' words and does them is like a wise man who builds his house on rock. But the man who hears but does not do is like a man who builds his house on sand and then watches it become all washed away by the spring rains and floods (7:24-27).

Matthew is determined to leave his readers with no uncertainty that this is a main point of his gospel. To clinch his argument, the last judgment scene in 25:31-46 is placed at the climax of his gospel: it contains the last words of Jesus before the passion narrative begins. The audience for the judgment is all the nations of the world. The matter for judgment is how each person has treated the hungry, the thirsty, the stranger, and the prisoner. The final sentence is based on what a disciple has actually *done* for these people. A fourfold repetition of the word *do* makes this as emphatic as possible: "As often as you did it for one of my least brothers, you did it for me" (25:40). "As often as you neglected to do it to one of these least ones, you neglected to do it to me" (25:45).

However, in the last judgment scene, Matthew does more than present this broad direction of loving service. He is very anxious to point out the small concrete details of daily life in which this love is shown. In so doing, he is drawing on a tradition that goes back to imitation of Jesus himself. Here we can take some examples from Jesus' Sermon on the Mount which are especially directed to Christian teachers. I say this because Jesus mentions specifically in 5:19 those who live by his directions and *teach others.*

Although this love is outwardly exhibited in many ways, most important is the matter of first cleansing the heart of hatred and anger through sincere forgiveness. The inner heart can never be just indifferent or complacent. To bring this out, Jesus repeats again and again— eight times in the Sermon on the Mount (Matt. 5-7)—the phrase *your brother.* The important matter is an affectionate love and concern for each person as a brother or sister. The exterior commandment, "You shall not commit murder," is significant, but Jesus goes to the roots of anger that are found in the heart and are shown in abusive words as well. They are the beginnings of the exterior act of murder: "What I say to you is: everyone who grows angry with his brother shall be liable to judgment; any man who uses abusive language toward his brother shall be answerable to the Sanhedrin, and if he holds him in contempt he risks the fires of Gehenna" (5:22). In practice then, even if a person is engaged in a most solemn act of worship, yet there he remembers that his brother has something against him, he should drop everything and go to talk with him (5:23-24).

In regard to sexual behavior, the same concern for the inner heart is present. The exterior commandment says "You shall not commit adultery." However, even looks are important because they betray thoughts and desires: "What I say to you is: anyone who looks lustfully at a woman has already committed adultery with her in his thoughts" (Matt. 5:28).

Another of the ten commandments concerns false oaths and lying to one's neighbor. Here once again it is interior trust and fidelity to one's neighbor that is exemplified in speech. There is really no need for oaths and swearing of any kind. Simple and truthful speech means that when you say "yes" you mean it, and the same with "no." "Say 'Yes' when you mean 'Yes' and 'No' when you mean 'No.' Anything beyond that is from the evil one" (Matt. 5:37).

Everyday life means facing injustice and suffering harm from those who take advantage of their position of power, influence, or money. In Jesus' time, hundreds of laws, Roman and Jewish, provided ways to obtain justice from the courts or government in the face of abused rights. The expression, "An eye for an eye, a tooth for a tooth" (Matt. 5:38; Exod. 21:24) was an idiom that was never literally applied. It was meant to express that proper indemnity should be made, rather than indulging in angry retaliation which might go far beyond the matter at hand. But Jesus provides a new way to face injustice: to retaliate with love! "But what I say to you is: offer no resistance to injury. When a person strikes you on the right cheek, turn and offer him the other" (Matt. 5:39). For Jesus these were not theories or ideals, but the expression of his own personal practice. As we have seen, he offered no resistance to Judas and those who came to arrest him. Luke describes him as even healing one of the soldiers (Luke 22:51).

Jesus well realizes that his own way is ridiculous according to human standards ("ridiculous"—a matter for laughing, in its root meaning). So he describes in humorous terms this way of love so foreign to everyday behavior. We might paraphrase his saying to read "If someone wants to bring you to court and sue for your shirt, offer him your coat also" (Matt. 5:40). Jesus' way of love is meant to be a surprise and shock to the world. Again, it was common practice in those days for Roman authorities, especially the military, to commandeer civilians to help carry provisions and baggage along the road. Anger and resentment are the usual expected response after a long journey under the hot sun with a heavy burden. Yet the follower of Jesus, the true teacher, carries it out of love and at the end even smiles and offers to do more! "Should anyone press you into service for one mile, go with him two miles" (5:41).

Yet the reality of life is that there are people who do not like us and even hurt us—the "enemy." Jesus provides an unusual but practical way to deal with this. It is to "retaliate" with a blessing and continual prayer for "enemies" every time we think about them. "My command to you is: love your enemies, pray for your persecutors" (Matt. 5:44).

When this type of unconditional love appears on earth, it is the surest sign of God's presence; it is God himself in action: "This will prove that you are sons of your heavenly Father, for his sun rises on the bad and the good, he rains on the just and the unjust" (5:45). This type of outflowing love shows itself even on the street or "sidewalk." The loving person does not hesitate to greet the stranger, for everyone is his brother: "If you love those who love you, what merit is there in that? Do not tax collectors do as much? And if you greet your brothers only, what is so praiseworthy about that? Do not pagans do as much?" (5:46-47).

Jesus' way of love even extends to the way we speak about others or "rate" them. "If you want to avoid judgment, stop passing judgment" (7:1). Judging others interferes with the heart of love which is acceptance and forgiveness. Jesus says, "Your verdict on others will be the verdict passed on you" (7:2). The one who judges is revealing more about himself than about the other person. Instead of constantly evaluating others and comparing ourselves to others, we should honestly search ourselves—not in a condemnatory fashion—in order to be aware of what we are. "Why look at the speck in your brother's eye when you miss the plank in your own? How can you say to your brother, 'Let me take that speck out of your eye,' while all the time the plank remains in your own? You hypocrite! Remove the plank from your own eye first; then you will see clearly to take the speck from your brother's eye" (7:3-5).

We can see, then, that Matthew considers it absolutely essential that the teacher communicate Jesus' message through action, even more than by words. He is especially thinking about teachers as he recalls Jesus' words, "Be on your guard against false prophets, who come to you in sheep's clothing but underneath are wolves on the prowl. You will know them by their deeds" (7:15-16).

To sum up: *We can state that Matthew is especially concerned that church teachers model themselves on Jesus as teacher. Jesus taught with authority and brought men to God through personal contact. Matthew's church, through Jesus' presence, possesses the same power and authority in its leaders and teachers. They are responsible for teaching and baptizing others. Matthew emphasizes the authority of legitimate church leaders because he is concerned with the transmission and preservation of the authentic tradition about Jesus in the face of serious opposition.*

# 15. Luke, Acts—A Living Succession of Teachers

As we all know, Luke is the author of a two-volume work, the Acts of the Apostles and the gospel bearing his name. In Acts he writes that his previous volume was intended to tell about "all that Jesus did and taught until the day he was taken up" (Acts 1:1-2). In the same chapter, he outlines the scope of his second volume. He will trace the spread of the gospel from Jerusalem, Judea, and Samaria to the ends of the earth (Acts 1:8). (The "ends of the earth" may refer to Rome, the center of the Empire.)

For Luke, as well as for the other gospel writers, teaching means instruction and guidance in a new way of life. One of his favorite terms is *the Way*. He describes Apollos as a man instructed, *katēchoumenos*, in the Way of the Lord (Acts 18:25). Apollos' later learning about the resurrection from Aquila and Priscilla is described as a more accurate instruction in the Way of God (18:26). Before his conversion, Paul persecuted members of the Way (9:2; 24:14). In explaining this to the Roman governor Felix while on trial at Caesarea, Paul relates that he worships the God of his Fathers "according to the Way, which they call a sect" (24:14).

From reading the first chapters of Acts we find specific information as to what Luke meant by "the Way." He is thinking in terms of a special way of living that is characteristic of Jesus' followers. The indications are brief but pregnant with meaning. The earliest Christians were especially united in "the apostles' instruction and the communal life, . . . the breaking of the bread and the prayers" (2:42). The next verses add some details. The community used to meet together for special meals in various homes; the members shared their possessions with one another, even selling their property to help those who were in need. Together they went to the Temple for prayers.

The description of this way of life immediately follows the story of the first baptism of new members. Hence it is quite certain that baptism meant initiation into a community that shared this distinctive life-style. Some made heroic sacrifices in order to participate to the full in the life of the commune. The goal of the community was that there should not be a poor person among them (Acts 4:34). Luke singles out Barnabas, a Levite from Cyprus, as an outstanding example. This man sold a large piece of land and brought the money to the apostles, the leaders of the community.

The community was not centered on itself. Its members felt an urgent responsibility not only to tell people about the resurrection of Jesus (Acts 4:33), but actively to help the poor outside their community. Food and goods were distributed daily to widows—a project which eventually reached such proportions that the apostles appointed seven assistants to help with it (6:1-6).

While all this does not tell us directly about the teachers, it certainly indicates that they must have been outstanding men who could actively initiate new converts into such a manner of life. Barnabas, who is named among the prophets and teachers later on at Antioch (Acts 13:1), would have been such a teacher. As we have seen above, Luke makes special mention of his extraordinary generosity.

With this Lukan picture of the early Christians in mind, we can understand why the evangelist places such special emphasis on the concrete details of the Christian life. He is speaking from experience. He knows that such instruction is needed for those who would join the Way. For this reason, he gives special attention in his gospel to the importance of the present ethical demands of the Good News. For example, only Luke records the specific directions that the Baptist gave to various groups who asked him, "What ought we to do?" (3:10): "'Let the man with two coats give to him who has none. The man who has food should do the same.' Tax collectors also came to be baptized, and they said to him, 'Teacher, what are we to do?' He answered them, 'Exact nothing over and above your fixed amount.' Soldiers likewise asked him . . .

He told them, 'Don't bully anyone . . . Be content with your pay'" (Luke 3:10, 11-14).

From experience Luke knew that the matter of money and possessions was a great obstacle for converts. Hence he gives more attention to this question than any of the other gospel writers, laying down stringent requirements for discipleship. A convert must be ready to sell *all* that he has in order to meet the needs of the poor (18:22). The beatitudes as given in Luke, in contrast to Matthew, stress the actual condition of voluntary poverty rather than "spiritual poverty." Luke's version is "Blest are you poor . . . " (6:20) and "woe to you rich" (6:24). Only Luke recalls the story of the rich man and Lazarus (16:19-31), and the parable of the man who faced sudden death after a life of amassing riches (12:13-21). And, obviously, the story of the good Samaritan (10:29-37) presents the example of a man who went all the way to respond to someone in desperate need: he carried him to an inn, took personal care of him, and even left a considerable sum of money to insure that the man would receive the best of attention. The parable concludes with the words, "Go, and do in like manner." Luke leaves no doubt that this story is to be put into active practice by those who aspire to be Christians.

In his presentation of Jesus, there are good reasons to believe that Luke is thinking of Jesus as a model for the teacher in the church. More than any other gospel he uses the term *didaskalos*, teacher, to refer to Jesus. The introductory call of the disciples is meant to show that the early church continues the teaching word of Jesus. The story begins with Jesus teaching the crowd by the lake. Later, when Jesus directs Peter to lower his nets for a catch of fish, Simon replies that he has been fishing all night without success, but *at Jesus' word*, they will lower the nets again. When they do so, they enclose such a multitude of fish that the two boats are filled almost to the sinking point. The symbolism brings out the idea that Simon and the others will continue the work of Jesus, preaching by the power of his word. This is confirmed by the concluding words of Jesus, "Do not be afraid, from now on you will be catching men" (5:10).

One special Lukan emphasis on Jesus as a model for teachers should be given particular attention: the love he showed toward strangers.

Luke, like Matthew, highlights the story of Jesus' cure of a Roman centurion's servant (Luke 7:1-10; Matt. 8:5-13). However, in Luke, Jesus not only offers to go to his house (as in Matthew); he actually sets out toward the house and is only a short distance away when the centurion sends his friends to meet him. Only Luke draws attention to the good qualities and deeds of the centurion: the Jewish elders tell Jesus, "He deserves this favor from you, because he loves our people, and even built our synagogue for us" (Luke 7:5). At Nazareth, Jesus reminds his Jewish brethren that some of the greatest miracles in the Old Testament were performed for Gentiles: the resurrection of the dead son of the widow of Zarephath near Sidon, and the cure of Naaman the Syrian from leprosy (2 Kings 5).

Again, the Samaritans, as half-Jews, were regarded as foreigners by strict Jews. Despite this, in his parable of the good Samaritan, Jesus uses a Samaritan as an example of the ultimate in love (Luke 10:25-37). He cures a Samaritan leper, who proves to be the most grateful of those healed (17:11-19), even though he is a "foreigner" (17:18). Jesus enters a Samaritan town on the way to Jerusalem and rebukes his disciples when they are angry because they were not welcomed (9:51-56). Jesus reserves some of his most beautiful last words for a stranger, a criminal crucified at his side (23:43).

It is very significant that, after the death of Jesus, two of his disciples met him in the form of a stranger walking along the road. Although they talked with him and finally invited him to share a meal, it is only after they break bread together that they recognize the Risen Jesus (Luke 24:13-35). His final words in Luke direct the disciples to bring the Good News to the whole Gentile world: "In his name, penance for the remission of sins is to be preached to all the nations, beginning at Jerusalem" (24:47). The gospel of Luke is a great manifesto of God's love for the entire world, a love that actively works to break down the barriers that separate groups from one another. Jesus is the agent of this love— a model for the Christian teacher who is shown as putting this directive into practice in the book of the Acts of the Apostles.

Another dominant concern in Luke-Acts yields important information about teachers in the early church. The author's intention, to trace the unbroken succession of teachers[30] and tradition back to Jesus himself, is apparent right from the beginning of Acts. Luke outlines the mission of the earthly Jesus: all that he began to do and teach (Acts 1: 1-2) and notes how Jesus presented himself alive to the Eleven for forty days before his ascension. Then, after describing Jesus' ascension "from the mount called Olivet," and the apostles' return to the upper room in Jerusalem (Acts 1:9-13), Luke gives their names just as these are listed in his gospel, only omitting "Judas Iscariot who turned traitor" (Luke 6:14-16). He evidently wants to trace the post-pentecostal community back to the Twelve, and through the Twelve to Jesus himself. This is why it is stated that the qualification for the election of a successor to Judas must be someone who was with Jesus right from the time of John the Baptist (Acts 1:15-22).

Luke then continues this theme of *apostolic succession* all through Acts. He wants to show that it is the Twelve, especially Peter, who are ultimately, even if indirectly, responsible for the universal spread of the church to the Gentile world. This is indicated through the appointment of the seven "deacons" as assistants to the Twelve. These seven, scattered by persecution, bring the gospel to Samaria, Africa, and Antioch (8:1-40; 11:19-20). Luke also shows clearly that the decision to admit Gentile converts without circumcision goes back to Peter and the conversion of Cornelius (chapters 10-11).

Only when Peter has made this fundamental decision will Luke tell about Paul's work in the Gentile world. He even tries to establish a link between Paul and the Twelve by relating how Barnabas took Paul to the apostles in Jerusalem after his conversion (Acts 9:27). The theme of succession continues as Paul appoints presbyters in Lystra, Iconium, and Antioch (14:23). The succession motif is completed as Paul, feeling that he will never see the presbyters at Ephesus again, gives them a farewell last testament, admonishing them to carry on his work (20:17-38).

As we have pointed out in other connections, this "tradition" or succession of teachers is by no means a mere passing on of information from one teacher to another. It is a *lived* tradition passed on in the very lives of the teachers themselves. Luke is careful to indicate how both Peter and Paul continue and duplicate the powerful actions of Jesus. In the cure of the paralytic Aeneas (Acts 9:33-34), and in the raising of the widow Tabitha at Joppa (9:36-41), Peter heals in the same manner and almost with the same words as Jesus himself. Luke heightens the parallelism by including in the latter story many of the same details as the gospel narrative of the raising of Jairus' daughter: e.g., the words of the cure, Peter's action in taking the woman by the hand, and the prohibition of bystanders (cf. Luke 8:51-56).

In describing Paul's life, Luke continues the same parallelism. The apostle cures a man at Lystra who was a cripple from birth (Acts 14: 8-10). He also raises up a young man called Eutychus who was believed to be dead after falling from a window while listening to one of Paul's long sermons (20:1-10). In Acts, Luke again brings out the importance of tradition as being a matter that is *lived* in those who pass it on. Such a tradition—a manner of life characteristic of Jesus himself—is referred to by Paul in his address to the presbyters at Ephesus. He asks them to recall his manner of life among them (20:18). He goes into specifics: enduring persecution (20:19), preaching from house to house (20:20), never asking for money or clothes but supporting himself by the work of his own hands (20:33-34). This tradition is traced to Jesus himself by a quotation of his actual words: "You need to recall the words of the Lord Jesus himself, who said, 'There is more happiness in giving than receiving'" (20:35).

In the Acts of the Apostles, most of the teaching appears to be directed to the newly baptized or to outsiders who are interested, at least to some extent, in becoming Christians. Teaching takes place in the Temple (4:1-2; 5:21, 25), throughout Jerusalem (5:28), in homes (5:42). Paul and Barnabas taught for a whole year at Antioch, where most of their audience would have been catechumens, or newly baptized (11: 25-26), since the church there had been in existence only a short time (11:19-22).

Luke tells us that Paul taught for more than a year and a half at Corinth (Acts 18:11) and for more than two years at Ephesus (19:8-10). Here the work was surely among new converts, since Paul first brought the gospel to these places. The last words of Acts tell us that Paul continued to teach at Rome "about the Lord Jesus Christ." These references bring out the special direction of teaching to those who were first learning what it meant to be a Christian. Here, especially, was a need for teachers who would present—through their own actions—a dynamic pattern of Christian living.

It should also be noted that the Acts of the Apostles forms an important sequel and follow-up to Luke's gospel's emphasis on the initiative and love Jesus showed toward strangers. This is because Luke is especially sensitive to the oneness of God. For Luke, God, being one, actively creates oneness among human persons, breaking down divisive barriers everywhere on earth through his Spirit. Consequently, we find Christian teachers and leaders actively promoting oneness, real community, through their example and lives. We have seen that under the "teaching of the Twelve" the first Christian community had economic and social community through sharing possessions and goods so that no one would be in need. In a beautiful summary Luke writes, "The community of believers were of one heart and one mind. None of them ever claimed anything as his own; rather, everything was held in common" (Acts 4:32). Their religious and spiritual unity was particularly evident when they broke bread in their homes in memory of Jesus and prayed in the Temple together (2:46).

Christian teachers and leaders are also shown as fostering this unity in the Spirit of God by their approach to strangers and outsiders. Philip brings the Good News to the Samaritans who are baptized and receive the Spirit, thus entering into community with Peter and John and their Jewish brothers (Acts 8:9-25). Peter and John continue Philip's work by going to other Samaritan villages (8:25).

In the Acts of the Apostles, the Spirit is explicitly mentioned whenever such striking demonstrations of bringing persons into community take place. Thus, directed by the Spirit, Philip brings the Good News to an Ethiopian returning to Africa (8:26-40).

Again, through the special intervention of God and the work of the Spirit, Peter is led to visit the home of Cornelius, a Roman centurion (10:1-48)—an action which defied all the Jewish customs and food regulations that made it "impossible" for Jew and Gentile to associate with one another. When Peter and his Jewish companions arrive at the home of Cornelius and speak to the assembled Gentiles, the Holy Spirit comes down on the whole group of Jews and Gentiles just as at the first Pentecost (10:44). This was a great surprise to the Jewish Christian believers

(10:45) and a complete shock to the Jerusalem community when they heard about it. Some even took issue with Peter about the matter: "As a result, when Peter went up to Jerusalem, some among the circumcised took issue with him, saying, 'You entered the house of uncircumcised men and ate with them'" (11:3). Peter can only explain that he did so by the direct intervention of the Spirit of God.

Then, for the first time in the history of the world, as a result of the visit of Christian teachers, a joint Jewish-Gentile community was formed at Antioch in Syria, its members living and praying together on the basis of their common sharing in the Spirit of Jesus (Acts 11:19-21). The news of this phenomenon was such a complete surprise to the Jerusalem church that they sent their most faithful Barnabas to be with them. He and Paul stayed in that church a whole year, instructing new disciples (11:22-26). Because of this new unity, the community could not be called "Jews" or "Gentiles." For the first time its members were called "Christians" (11:26). It was at a worship service at Antioch that the Spirit directed that Paul and Barnabas were to be set aside for a new mission to the Gentile world to extend the new oneness in the Spirit that had been created in their own community (13:1-3).

*To sum up: For Luke, a believer is a follower of the "Way," a word that sums up the whole unique pattern of Christian life. Luke finds this pattern in the early church community with its extraordinary concern for the poor, its intense search for oneness and community along with its intense commitment of love and service to outsiders. The Christian* didaskalos *or teacher is a person who lives and acts in the name of Jesus so intensely that he or she is a living successor of Jesus himself.*

# 16.  John—Criteria for an
Authentic Teacher

The gospel of John was written to answer a burning question of his time, and our time as well: Is there a real difference between a *Christian teacher* and other teachers? A crucial point in John's time was the matter of the authenticity and power of Jesus' teaching as carried on in the church. "How did this man get his education when he had no teacher?" (7:15) was a pointed question addressed not only to Jesus in the gospel but to the church. In those days, just as in our own time, it was most important to have "teaching credentials." In Jewish thought, authenticity or credentials of teaching were traced back from disciple to master through the centuries to Moses himself, who had learned from God. The gradual separation of the church from official Judaism naturally resulted in a break with the authoritative teaching of the synagogue. Consequently, it was most important to establish new credentials for teaching in the church.

The problem becomes much clearer when we review the historical circumstances under which the gospel of John was written. The fourth gospel was put into its final form at least toward the end of the first century.[31] An important apologetic concern of the author was to defend and encourage *the church*, especially its Jewish members who were facing new challenges from official Judaism. This situation was one of the effects of the Jewish War with Rome which destroyed Jerusalem about 70 A.D. As mentioned earlier, after that tragic time, the Pharisees emerged as the most powerful group in Judaism and succeeded in reforming Judaism around Pharisaic ideals and, as a result, the diversity present in Judaism during the time of Jesus gradually disappeared. Little by little, the new official Judaism began to take a much more definite stand against Christians, so that Jewish Christians found it difficult to attend the synagogue and live at peace with their Jewish brothers.

John's gospel shows many marks of this struggle. Over seventy times, the author refers to "the Jews," almost as if Jesus himself were not a Jew. Most of the time the words are used in a hostile sense with particular reference to official Judaism. Since John's community was engaged in a struggle with this new Jewish leadership, John presents Jesus as experiencing the same conflict with the official Judaism of his day. This was not by any means a struggle with Israel or the Jewish people. Throughout the gospel, it is clear that "salvation is from the Jews" (4:22), i.e., from Jerusalem and official Jewish leadership both in the time of Jesus and in the time of John. It is within the context of confrontation with official Judaism that the question of authentic teaching becomes crucial. Are there new authoritative (in the sense of God's power being behind them) teachers to take the place of the Pharisees for Jewish Christians (as well as for Gentile Christians)?

John skillfully develops his response: God himself is the real *Teacher* of Israel, for it was he who taught Moses, the teacher of teachers. However, in Jesus of Nazareth, God, the hidden Teacher of Israel, was so truly at work that they were actually one with each other. At the resurrection, Jesus became openly manifest as the teacher-God of Israel. At the same time, he communicated his Spirit to his disciples so that they could continue to teach exactly as he had taught and with the same power. The core of their teaching was a living tradition of imitation of Jesus and faithful transmission of his words and directives. It was not, however, a matter of individual powers but a particular gift given to someone within a community which itself was inspired by the Paraclete, the Holy Spirit of Jesus. It was a community, moreover, guided by new pastors and leaders in place of the older Jewish leadership.

GOD TEACHING IN JESUS AND HIS DISCIPLES

John provides a very definite literary clue to his pattern of thought. He uses the device known as *inclusion*, the repetition of a theme at the beginning and end of a work. In the gospel of John, the first words of Jesus' disciples when they meet him at the Jordan are, "Rabbi (which means *Teacher*), where do you stay?" (1:38). At the end of the book, the first words of his disciple, Mary Magdalen, are almost the same (but with a progression in meaning): "'Rabbouni!' (which means 'Teacher')" (20:16).

This teacher is hidden in Israel—in the sense that he is unrecognized and unknown. Already in John 1:26, John the Baptist states that there is someone in their midst whom they do not know. The crowds at the Feast of Tabernacles say that when the Messiah has come, no one will know where he is from, yet they know the origins of Jesus. Jesus replies that his origin is indeed mysterious because it is from God (7:28). The story of the blind man appears to reflect the same theme in the Pharisees' statement: "We know that God spoke to Moses, but we have no idea where this man comes from" (9:29). The conclusion of John's "Book of Signs" (chapters 1-12) seems to bring this theme to a climax when John writes that Jesus departed and hid himself from the people after a final appeal confirmed by a voice from heaven (12:27-36). Pilate's question, "Where do you come from?" (19:9) can only be answered after Jesus' resurrection.

The progression from understanding Jesus as a teacher from God to believing in him as a teacher-God is carefully developed by the author. The first chapter of John has a whole list of titles ascribed to Jesus, beginning with Rabbi or Teacher (1:38), and continuing with Messiah (1:41), Son of God, and King of Israel (1:49). At the end of the chapter, John has Jesus promise a fuller revelation of these titles when he proclaims that the heavens will be opened and the angels of God will ascend and descend upon the Son of Man (1:51).

In the discourse with Nicodemus (John 3:1-21), a deliberate contrast is made between the ordinary "teacher of Israel" (3:10) and the true teacher of Israel who is from God (3:2), who speaks in terms of the Spirit (3:5-8), and whose origin from God will be proved by his ascension (3:11-15). In the bread discourse (chapter 6), Jesus proclaims that the prophecy of Isaiah, "Your sons shall be taught by the Lord" (Isaiah 54:13), will be fulfilled in him as a teacher, because anyone who has learned from the Father will come to him (John 6:45-46). In John 8:28-

29, Jesus makes the striking statement, "When you lift up the Son of Man, you will come to realize that I AM and that I do nothing by myself. I say only what the Father has taught me." This points to Jesus' ascension as a certification of his union with the Father, especially as a teacher.

Only the resurrection of Jesus makes it no longer hidden but evident that he is the teacher-God of Israel. As was said earlier, the first appearance of Jesus to Mary Magdalen brings this out, as her first word "'Rabbouni!' (which means 'Teacher')" (John 20:16) echoes the first words of the first disciple of Jesus (1:38). These words gain their full impact, I believe, when considered in the context of Isaiah (30:19-20): "O people of Zion, who dwell in Jerusalem; no more will you weep; He will be gracious to you when you cry out, as soon as he *hears* he will answer you. The *Lord* will give you the bread you need and the water for which you thirst. No longer will your *Teacher hide* himself, but with your own eyes you shall see your Teacher . . .''

In this text, it is God himself who is the hidden Teacher of Israel revealing himself to repentant Zion who weeps and calls out to him for help. The striking parallels to Mary Magdalen in John 20 will immediately be noticed: she is weeping outside the tomb because her Lord has been taken away. At first she does not recognize him in the figure of the gardener. However, she hears his voice and turns (a hint of the biblical sense of turning or conversion). Only then does she see him as the Lord (John 20:18) and call him *Rabbouni* or Teacher.

We have yet to indicate why John's audience would see a connection between the resurrection of Jesus and his manifestation as teacher-God. John carefully explains this link by developing the full implication of Jesus' mission as the final prophet to the world. Even in the Hebrew Scriptures, the prophet had a certain aura of God about him. As one sent by God, there was "something of God" surrounding the prophet's person. For example, the prophet spoke to the people with definitive statements as a direct mouthpiece of God, even speaking in the first person: "Thus says the Lord, '*I* am about to do such and such.'" To receive a prophet was to receive God himself; to reject a prophet was to reject God (2 Kings 17:10-16; 1 Sam. 15:1-23). Extraordinary signs often accompanied the prophet's words, since the power of the sender went with his messenger. For example, God directed Moses to work signs before the people so that his words would be proved to be those of the powerful God who sent him. Moses did so and the people believed in God (Exod. 4:29-31).

The careers of the prophets Elijah and Elishah (1 Kings 17-2 Kings 9) illustrate the atmosphere of God's power that surrounded a prophet according to popular thinking. The two prophets multiplied bread and oil, healed the sick, and even raised the dead. In fact, this transfer of God's word and power to the messenger-prophet appeared so complete at times that he seemed to be almost a double to represent God himself to the people. This was based on the example of Moses who spoke in God's own name to Pharaoh (Exod. 5:23). Prophets who came after him would speak in his name to such a degree that if the people did not respond, God himself would make them answer for it (Deut. 18:15-20).

This scriptural background is an important foundation for John's presentation of Jesus as the teacher-prophet-God. Jesus is a prophet, and, as such, God's messenger in word and deed. Yet, he is God's final messenger of the last *times*. Hence, *all* God's power and word are manifest in him, and *all* of God's titles can be transferred to him.[32] He is, then, Son of God in the fullest sense of the word. John leaves no loopholes in presenting this argument. First of all, Jesus is commonly represented in this gospel as a prophet. The key verb "send" is used some forty times to describe Jesus' relationship to the Father. This word is found in the description of each of the Old Testament prophets. Jesus is also specifically called a prophet by both the converted blind man and the Samaritan woman (John 4:19; 9:17).

But the unique matter is that Jesus is God's long-expected *final* prophet. At the multiplication of the loaves, the crowds exclaim that Jesus is the prophet who is to come into the world (John 6:14). At the Feast of Tabernacles, when Jesus promises the gift of living water, some people respond, "This is really the prophet" (7:40). A key text is found in John 10:34. The Jews had taken up stones to cast at Jesus because of his statement: "The Father and I are one." They based their action on Jesus' claim to make himself God (10:33). Jesus replies: "Is it not written in your law, 'I have said, You are gods'? If it calls those men gods to whom God's word was addressed—and Scripture cannot lose its force—do you claim that I blasphemed when, as he whom the Father consecrated and sent into the world, I said, 'I am God's Son'?" (10:34-36). Jesus' complete sanctification and mission in the world as God's final envoy and prophet merits his appropriation of the title of Son of God.

The resurrection and exaltation of Jesus is the final seal of this title. If Jesus is a true prophet, his proclamation about the imminent coming of the kingdom and the eschatological age must be true. This would have to be vindicated by God in some way after his death. For a Jew of the time, many signs both in the cosmic and human realm could point to this. However, one final and infallible sign or proof would be the resurrection of a just man. This was a phenomenon reserved for the last days (according to Jewish belief), as witnessed in Martha's response to Jesus in reference to Lazarus her brother: "I know that he will rise again in the resurrection on the last day" (John 11:24). Jesus' own resurrection witnessed by his disciples in various apparitions seals his word that the last times, the dawn of a new age, have indeed come. Jesus is a true prophet—God's final prophet in so complete a way that he can state: "The Father and I are one" (10:30).

Once Jesus has shown himself to be teacher-God with all the authority implicit in this title, the next step is to communicate his Spirit to his community of disciples so they can be authentic teachers like himself. His first words are a transfer of his own mission to his community, "As the Father has sent me, so I send you" (John 20:21). Then, just as God breathed on the first man so that he became a living being from God (Gen. 2:7; cf. 1 Cor. 15:45), Jesus breathes upon his disciples and says, "Receive the Holy Spirit. If you forgive men's sins, they are forgiven them; if you hold them bound, they are held bound" (John 20:23).

This forgiveness or binding of sin is closely connected with the teaching authority of the church. Similar words are found in the context of the promise made to Peter as the rock of the church (Matt. 16:19) and also in reference to the power within the Christian community to admit or exclude the sinner (Matt. 18:18). The teacher is intimately connected with the whole matter of the requirements of admission or exclusion from the Christian community and the qualifications of membership. The words "binding and loosing" also have a rabbinic background referring to the power of the teacher to make decisions about the law.

## THE COMMUNICATION OF AUTHENTIC TEACHING

John is deeply concerned to show that there is a living tradition of authentic teaching that has come from the Father, to Jesus, to his disciples, and so to the church. The first step in this living tradition is Jesus' own imitation of the Father, which we have already studied. The second step in this living tradition is that the disciples have learned from Jesus himself and become like him in his imitation of the Father. John sums up this ideal of imitation in his Last Supper account of the washing of the disciples' feet. Jesus' action in stripping his garments and washing their feet symbolizes his whole life of service. If they call him "Teacher and Lord" (13:13), it is because he has been a true teacher whose example they can follow: "But if I washed your feet—I who am Teacher and Lord—then you must wash each other's feet. What I just did was to give you an example; as I have done, so you must do" (13:14-15). The only mark of true discipleship will be the performance of these same deeds by his followers. Merely to know about them will not be enough (13:16-17).

The third step in the line of teaching tradition takes place as Jesus' disciples continue Jesus' mission by forming a community of believers. The first words of the Risen Jesus to the disciples are: "As the Father has sent me, so I send you" (John 20:21). Again, wherever they go they will be full representatives of Jesus. Those who receive them will be receiving Jesus himself (13:20). They will continue to perform Jesus' works; in fact, they will perform even greater ones (14:12). The unmistakable mark of the authentic community of Jesus will be the mutual love and unity of its members which will move the world to belief; "That all may be one as you, Father, are in me, and I in you; I pray that they may be [one] in us, that the world may believe that you sent me . . . I living in them, you living in me—that their unity may be complete. So shall the world know that you sent me, and that you loved them as you loved me" (17:21,23).

This third step is made possible only by a dynamic inner agent, the Holy Spirit or Paraclete. If we examine the Paraclete's function in chapters 14-16, we find that what he does is to make it possible for the believer to continue the work of Jesus. For example, he is the Spirit of truth (John 14:17), just as Jesus is the truth (14:6). He helps men bear witness (15:26-27), just as Jesus bore witness. He comes from the Father (15:26), just as Jesus came from the Father (16:28). He teaches, recalling Jesus' words (14:26) just as Jesus taught. In effect, the Paraclete is really a "double" of Jesus.[33] He lives in believers recalling Jesus' word and effectively helping them to practice it as an example to the world. In this way people will be able truly to understand what it means to live the life of Christ in a new age and in new circumstances. Thus, the community itself is an authentic living testimony to Jesus as its members reflect on his word and put it into action.

Although, because of the working of the Spirit, no one in the church plays a "subordinate" role, the gospel does point to the leaders of the church as having an essential part. They manifest the presence of Jesus by being good shepherds to their community, in the same way that Jesus himself was a good shepherd to his own first flock. The figure of Peter in the fourth gospel appears to be a model for this type of church leadership. The gospel ends with Peter himself being commissioned by Jesus to act as a shepherd of the church. He shows himself a true shepherd by voluntarily going as far as death in order to fulfill his ministry and become perfectly like his master (John 21:15-19). Thus he portrays in action the love of Jesus the good shepherd. Because of this emphasis on Peter as shepherd, it is probable that the parables of the good shepherd in chapter 10 are especially directed toward leaders of the Christian community.

To sum up: *The matter of authentic teaching is an essential concern of the fourth gospel. With the break from the synagogue, John is concerned to establish a genuine authoritative source of teachers and teaching that goes back to the disciples of Jesus, to Jesus himself, and from Jesus to God. It is authoritative in the sense that God is the author, first in Jesus as teacher-God, and secondly in the Paraclete, the Holy Spirit working in the Christian teaching community. John would say that the Christian teacher of any time is really different and unique. His credentials go back to Jesus and to God through the inner powerful activity of the Paraclete that prompts him to become a "double" for Jesus.*

# 17. "Don't Become a Teacher"— The Letter of James

If we could be sure that this letter was personally written by James, "brother" of Jesus and the first bishop of Jerusalem, the letter would have extraordinary authority and clearly would have been written before his martyrdom around 62 A.D. However, this authorship and date are much disputed among scholars.[34] The document may have been written in the name of James by another author in order to give his letter special attention.

It is quite important to note that, as a teacher, the author draws heavily upon a tradition about Jesus. In this short letter, some forty-eight verses show the influence of the Sermon on the Mount (or the tradition behind it), indicating that the author has carefully modeled his own life as a teacher upon that of Jesus himself. James, of course, would have been closest to Jesus, as a blood relative (Gal. 1:19).

For example, in the Sermon on the Mount, Jesus taught that we should use our tongues with utmost care especially in talking truthfully to our brothers from the heart. He had counselled against using oaths and swearing. "Say, 'Yes' when you mean 'Yes' and 'No' when you mean 'No'" (Matt. 5:37). Remembering the teaching of Jesus, James writes, "Above all else, my brothers, you must not swear an oath, any oath at all, either 'by heaven' or 'by earth.' Rather let it be 'yes' if you mean yes and 'no' if you mean no" (5:12).

Jesus had declared, "If you want to avoid judgment, stop passing judgment" (Matt. 7:1). James very carefully spells out the implications of this teaching for everyday actions: "Do not, my brothers, speak ill of one another. The one who speaks ill of his brother or judges his brother is speaking against the law. It is the law he judges. If, however, you judge the law you are no observer of the law, you are its judge. There is but one Lawgiver and Judge, one who can save and destroy. Who then are you to judge your neighbor?" (4:11-12).

Jesus had warned about living in the future and thinking about tomorrow, especially with regard to riches and material gains: "Enough, then, of worrying about tomorrow. Let tomorrow take care of itself" (Matt. 6:33). James develops this thought in detail: "Come now, you who say, 'Today or tomorrow we shall go to such and such a town, spend a year there, trade, and come off with a profit!' You have no idea what kind of life will be yours tomorrow. You are a vapor that appears briefly and vanishes" (4:13-14).

Indeed, no letter in the New Testament spells out as carefully as James' the picture of a teacher as a *doer* which is so much a part of the Sermon on the Mount and of the image of Jesus in Matthew's gospel. The writer's ideal is summed up in 1:22-24: "Act on this word. If all you do is listen to it, you are deceiving yourselves. A man who listens to God's word but does not put it into practice is like a man who looks into a mirror at the face he was born with; he looks at himself, then goes off and promptly forgets what he looked like."

Likewise, nowhere else in the New Testament are the practical effects of hearing the word described in such detail. For example, Christians should be "quick to hear, slow to speak, slow to anger; for a man's anger does not fulfill God's justice" (James 1:19-20). They should look after orphans and widows in their distress; this is part of true worship (1:27). But the greatest emphasis is on compassion and effective help for the poor and needy: "If a brother or sister has nothing to wear and no food for the day, and you say to them, 'Goodbye and good luck! Keep warm and well fed,' but do not meet their bodily needs, what good is that? So it is with the faith that does nothing in practice. It is thoroughly lifeless" (2:15-17).

We especially note what he has to say about teachers, since he speaks from experience (James 3:1). Because of the strict accountability of a teacher before God, few should aspire to the office. He humbly acknowledges that he himself as well as other teachers have often fallen short of the ideal (3:2). A teacher is in a unique position of influence because he can do so much to move people one way or another. The congregation is like a ship, and the teacher's tongue is like a rudder which gives it direction (3:4-5). It is like a spark which can set a whole forest afire (3:5).

Consequently, the author demands that teachers' lives be models for their listeners and students. They cannot use their tongues both to praise God in the liturgy and at the same time use them to curse men (James 3:10). If they do this, it shows that the inner person is not what he should be: "Does a spring gush forth fresh water and foul from the same outlet?" (3:11). A fig tree cannot produce olives, nor can a grapevine produce figs (3:12).

This inner purification, however, does not lead to mere silence or repression, especially of the tongue. It leads to a very positive use of speech to help oneself and others. When a Christian is suffering or in pain, instead of complaining, he/she should resort to intense prayer to God: "If anyone among you is suffering hardship, he must pray" (James 5:13). Times of special joy call for singing a song of God's praises: "If a person is in good spirits, he should sing a hymn of praise" (5:13). If a friend or neighbor is sick, the representatives of the church are to be called in to pray over the person with an anointing of oil. This is not only an outward cure but a prayer for the inner forgiveness that will transform the whole person (5:12-15). Indeed the tongue is the instrument of truth and thus can exhibit one of God's great attributes, that of truth: "Declare your sins to one another, and pray for one another, that you may find healing" (5:16). "The fervent petition of a holy man is powerful indeed" (5:16). Those who stray from the truth are not to be avoided or turned away from. On the contrary, they should be the object of the greatest love and concern: "My brothers, the case may arise among you of someone straying from the truth, and of another bringing him back. Remember this: the person who brings a sinner back from his way will save his soul from death and cancel a multitude of sins" (5:19-20).

To sum up: *The letter of James, then, underlines the basic importance of the tradition about Jesus, especially that contained in the Ser-*

*mon on the Mount. The tradition must be kept alive in the daily actions of the Christian. The author is a teacher and points out that this office implies the risk of greater judgment, since a teacher is responsible for the lives of others through his own example.*

# 18. "A Bishop Must Be Able to Teach"— The Pastoral Letters

The letters to Timothy and Titus are often called the Pastoral Letters because of their preoccupation with authentic teaching as handed down and guarded by an appointed church ministry. Whatever judgment we may make as to the extent of their Pauline authorship, they represent a final stage in the tendency we have already seen to emphasize an authentic succession of teaching going back to Jesus himself. In these letters, it is shown as a living tradition that can be traced from Jesus to Paul, and to the appointed leaders of the church. These latter are now a body of presbyter-bishops in which the teaching function has become centered.

In these letters, the "sound teaching," to use a favorite expression of the author, is found first in Jesus, then in Paul, then in the church leaders. The author carefully traces back all authentic teaching to Jesus. Authentic teaching is based on "the sound doctrines of our Lord Jesus Christ" (1 Tim. 6:3). It is the doctrine of God our Savior (Titus 2:10) whose grace has appeared in Jesus Christ to teach men to adopt a new way of life (Titus 2:11-14). This direction of life must be taught to others. Teaching and a new way of life are considered intimately united.

Paul himself has been especially called to manifest in his own life this grace of God. God has rescued him from his former ways in Judaism precisely so that he might be an *example* of this grace to others (1 Tim. 1:15-16). He has been called to be "preacher and apostle and teacher" (2 Tim. 1:11). It is this last function of *teacher* that especially concerns the author. Paul as teacher has left an authentic living tradition of both words and example that can be followed by Timothy and Titus, who are to guard it faithfully and hand it on to others.

This image of Paul as teacher by both word and example is not left open to any doubt. Timothy is warned in these words, "Remain faithful to what you have learned and believed, because you know *who your teachers were*" (2 Tim. 3:14). This teaching is embodied in a manner of life and conduct that Timothy and others have been able to witness. The author provides specific examples: "You have followed closely my teaching and my conduct. You have observed my resolution, fidelity, patience, love, and endurance, through persecutions and sufferings in Antioch, Iconium, and Lystra" (2 Tim. 3:10-11).

Next the author shows how this living tradition from Jesus, and then Paul, is to be found in Timothy and Titus and then handed on to others: "The things which you have heard from me through many witnesses you must hand on to trustworthy men who will be able to teach others" (2 Tim. 2:2). Once again, the matter of personal example is given special prominence: "Be a continuing example (*typos*) of love, faith, and purity to believers" (1 Tim. 4:12). Titus should be a model for the young men in his own good work as well as sound words so that opponents will find nothing evil they can say about him (Titus 2:7-9).

In this regard, Paul even advises Timothy to take a little wine once in a while for the sake of his stomach and frequent infirmities—instead of only drinking water (1 Tim. 5:23). While this may only be a health prescription, hints suggest that something more may be at stake. In the previous chapter, a warning was given about those who were forbidding marriage and requiring abstinence from certain foods. The author answers these false teachings by stating that all that God has created is good and is to be received with thanksgiving (1 Tim. 4:4). It is possible that some of this group abstained from wine out of fear of the body and its pleasures. The advice to Timothy may be a warning that nothing in his own life should even hint that he went along with such false teachings.

In reference to the trustworthy men to whom the authentic teaching is to be handed on, it is evident that the writer has in mind the appointed presbyter-bishops. I say presbyter-bishops because they appear to be a college or group heading the community. There is no indication that the writer is thinking of the monarchic type of hierarchy that first appears with Ignatius of Antioch in the second century. With Ignatius, the bishop or *episkopos* is the absolute leader of the community. He is assisted by a group of elders or *presbyteroi* who owe the bishop obedience. But the Pastoral Letters seem to imply a truly "collegial" form of church organization.

Paul orders Titus to appoint presbyters in all the towns of Crete. Since churches had already existed for many years on this island, they had their own leaders, perhaps by local election. The reason behind the new precept of appointment may be to strengthen the lines of teaching succession through Titus to Paul, and then to Jesus. The question of authentic teaching becomes so important in the face of errors that a strong effort was made to center it almost exclusively in the presbyter-bishops. Yet even here it is not a matter of their exclusive control of teaching but of their duty faithfully to guard the teaching and transmit it to others, above all by their lives.

For this reason, the qualifications for presbyter-bishops are centered in their personal conduct and example. Above all, the candidate for the office of bishop should be a good teacher, *didaktikos* (1 Tim. 3:2). As a teacher, his life should be a model that all can follow. Since he is to be a father whom his children in Christ can imitate, he must be a man who is known through his training of his own children. As a bishop, his home would be the center of church meetings, a place where the stranger from out of town would look first for hospitality (1 Tim. 3:1-7). The picture presented is that of the *small church*, a church that meets together in a home, where all are known to one another, and where the bishop is a man respected by everyone, including outsiders.

In view of this image of the presbyter-bishops as teachers, the author spells out the appropriate attitudes they should cultivate toward various groups within the church—the old, the young, widows, etc. Those presbyters who rule well are to be worthy of double honor, especially those who labor in the word and in *teaching* (1 Tim. 5:17). If their lives do not measure up to their teaching, they are to be openly confronted in the presence of the whole assembly (1 Tim. 5:20). This verse shows that the church leaders remain accountable for their lives not only to God but to the people they serve.

A few other points deserve attention. One is the crucial question of women and their place in the church. The Pastoral Letters preserve the most negative view on women in the New Testament, especially in their severe prohibition against women's teaching (cf. especially 1 Tim. 2:9-15). We will deal with this question in chapter 24.

In addition, the author is also strongly opposed to certain teachers who are pursuing their profession primarily in view of monetary considerations (1 Tim. 6:5). They are teaching in order to get "sordid gain" (Titus 1:11). We cannot draw elaborate conclusions from such brief information. However, it is evident that the author considers the teacher as a man who teaches because it is part of his own life-commitment; anyone with other predominant motives is betraying his vocation.

It should also be noted that the Hebrew Scriptures play an important role in all teaching. Paul reminds Timothy that from his childhood he has known the Scriptures. These can instruct unto salvation because of the faith in Jesus Christ to which they point. They are inspired and useful for teaching (2 Tim. 3:15-16). Timothy is told to be diligent in reading them publicly, in encouragement, and in teaching. Here we see that the reading of Scripture (as well as its interpretation and fulfillment in Christ) was essential to the work of the teacher.

To sum up: *The Pastoral Letters, like Luke and John, stress the succession of living tradition in the church. However, it is particularly embodied in the presbyter-bishops who seem to have absorbed the original teaching charisma into their office. Yet teaching is not a matter of the hierarchy's guarding and controlling a fixed body of doctrine or deposit of faith. It is an authentic tradition lived out by church leaders in such a way that their own lives proclaim it to others. "Sound teaching" is the life-style of Jesus himself, first learned by Paul, then by his disciples Timothy and Titus, then found in the presbyters and bishops.*

# 19. The First Letter of John—
# True and False Teachers

The author of this letter is gravely concerned about some Christian teachers whose teaching and way of life were very dangerous to the Christian community.[35] They have separated themselves from the community and probably formed new groups about themselves and their teaching: "It was from our ranks that they took their leave—not that they really belonged to us; for if they had belonged to us, they would have stayed with us" (1 John 2:19). These people had been prominent teachers, looked up to by others. They are called now "antichrists" (2:18) and "false prophets" (4:1,4).

The original audience knew very well what these false teachers taught and how they lived, but we have only hints scattered through this short letter. These are given by such expressions as "the man who claims" or "the one who" or by various contrasts. We can put these indications together to get some idea of their orientation. These opponents felt that they were light-filled beings in such intimate fellowship with God that they could no longer sin (1 John 1:6,8). They prized a deep inner "knowledge" or experience of God that was much more important than any exterior action (2:4). With such direct experience of God himself, they considered the human Jesus and his redemptory work, as well as his example, to be of minor importance. This last comes out by way of contrast, since the author has to state rather bluntly that a believer must hold that Christ has come in the flesh (4:2).

These references in the letter make us think that the "false" teachers were similar to, if not actually, gnostic-oriented Christians. The word "gnosis" means nothing more than "knowledge." But this particular kind of knowledge centers on the basic conviction that each person (or at least some persons) have a part of the divine nature within them. This is unrecognized by most people who are in ignorance of their true inner nature. To use gnostic terminology, they are "asleep" or "drunk." Thus they need to be awakened to know who they truly are and to be able to tap this powerful presence within them. This can only come about through a special kind of inner illumination or "gnosis."

Gnosticism can only be understood in terms of the world view it embraces: originally, there was only the one Light of God. It was through some kind of emanation of this Light (a primal man in some myths) that the world came into existence. However, in this process, the emanated Light or primal man became divided up, scattered, and imprisoned in human bodies. This was through the activity of a hostile creator and other evil spirits who originally came from the Light but somehow became separated from it. The world and the material universe were held captive by these spirits. The human body itself was under their control and served as a trap or prison for the divine sparks within that had originally come from the Light.

However, the Light never abandoned interest in the "lost sheep," the scattered particles of divine Light. It sent a redeemer or intermediary to liberate them. He did not come in human flesh, for then he would also have been in bondage and unable to help man. He came disguised as a human being and thus was able to deceive the evil spirits. The task of the messenger was to help men find out who they truly were and to teach them how to overcome the hostile cosmic powers and rejoin the true Light. Through this redeemer, they would be led to find out their true origin and obtain "salvation." This salvation was effected through an inner experience of the divine spark within them.

In the light of the strong gnostic influence within the Greek world of the time, we can understand why the author of 1 John is so concerned about Christian teachers who are intent on identifying Christianity with some inner experience of God or divine Light. In explaining the nature of a true Christian, 1 John gives us valuable insights as to how the presence of God can truly be recognized and what it means to be a real follower of Christ. In doing so, the author provides tests that can be applied to determine who is a true Christian teacher.

First of all, true Christian religion is not a matter of some inner illumination or experience that would make a person exempt from human weakness or sin. Rather, it is radical honesty and confession of sin that brings the forgiveness and love of God into our hearts. "If we say, 'We are free of the guilt of sin,' we deceive ourselves; the truth is not to be found in us. But if we acknowledge our sins, he who is just can be trusted to forgive our sins and cleanse us from every wrong" (1 John 1:8-9).

How, then, does a person know whether he is in the light? Claims or experiences are not enough. The important matter is "walking in the light," modeling one's actions on Jesus and his own loving service to men and women: "The way we can be sure we are in union with him is for the man who claims to abide in him to conduct himself just as he did . . . For the darkness is over and the real light begins to shine. The man who claims to be in light, hating his brother all the while, is in darkness even now. The man who continues in the light is the one who loves his brother" (1 John 2:5-6,8-10). For this reason, the letter strongly emphasizes the humanity of Jesus as a flesh and blood model of love that people can follow. "Every spirit that acknowledges Jesus Christ come in the flesh belongs to God" (4:2).

This Jesus is present in our hearts as an inner guide. The true Christian teacher leads a person to this inner teacher and does not try to lead him astray to follow himself: "I have written you these things about those who try to deceive you. As for you, the anointing you received from him remains in your hearts. This means you have no need for anyone to teach you. Rather, as his anointing teaches you about all things and is true . . ." (1 John 2:26-27).

The only way, then, to know who is a child of God, is to see if that person is like God himself in his love for each member of the human family: "That is the way to see who are God's children, and who are the devil's. No one whose actions are unholy belongs to God, nor anyone who fails to love his brother" (1 John 3:10). It is the only way to know if we are dead or alive: "That we have passed from death to life we know because we love the brothers. The man who does not love is among the living dead" (3:14). Inner attitudes are as important as external actions. To avoid murder and injury is not enough: "Anyone who hates his brother is a murderer, and you know that eternal life abides in no murderer's heart" (3:15).

This love has an unusual quality about it which immediately points to the divine presence, because it is like the love of Jesus himself in its intensity and totality: "The way we came to understand love was that he laid down his life for us; we too must lay down our lives for our brothers" (1 John 3:16). This kind of love is immediately evident because it always moves a person to take concrete visible steps to help the needy and poor: "I ask you, how can God's love survive in a man who has enough of this world's goods yet closes his heart to his brother when he sees him in need? Little children, let us love in deed and in truth and not merely talk about it" (3:17-18). Love of this kind makes prayer genuine and effective as coming from a clear conscience: "Beloved, if our consciences have nothing to charge us with, we can be sure that God is with us and that we will receive at his hands whatever we ask" (3:21-22).

This leads back again to the question as to how a person can "know" God. Knowledge and love do not first come from us, then to be directed to God. Love itself comes from God and flows through us to our brothers and sisters in the world: "Beloved, let us love one another because love is of God; everyone who loves is begotten of God and has knowledge of God. The man without love has known nothing of God, for God is love" (1 John 4:7-8). In other words, whenever this selfless outflow of love to others is found, there is God himself present and active. God showed this love in Jesus precisely that we might share it with him: "Love, then, consists in this: not that we have loved God, but that he has loved us and has sent his Son as an offering for our sins. Beloved, if God has loved us so, we must have the same love for one another. No one has ever seen God. Yet if we love one another, God dwells in us, and his love is brought to perfection in us" (4:10-12).

This brings the author to repeat once more the most startling definition of God in the entire Scriptures: "God is love, and he who abides in love abides in God, and God in him" (1 John 4:16). As a result, the crucial matter is surrender to this love, allowing it to flow through us in our daily actions: "We, for our part, love because he first loved us. If anyone says, 'My love is fixed on God,' yet hates his brother, he is a liar.

One who has no love for the brother he has seen cannot love the God he has not seen" (4:19-20).

To sum up: *The first letter of John was especially written to provide tests to distinguish between true and false Christian teachers. Those who teach religion essentially in terms of an inner mystical experience of their own or others have completely misunderstood the very nature of God himself: a burning love for all creation, especially each human being. Religion and contact with God mean that this love is absorbed through faith and then radiated out to others in ways that can be seen and felt by them. The true teacher is another Christ in action. For it is Jesus himself as supreme teacher who has understood God's love and shown it to others in his own life.*

# 20. Office, Role, and Charisma of the Teacher in the Early Church

Most of our information about teachers in the early church comes from Paul's letters. Teachers, *didaskoloi*, are named in 1 Corinthians as those who have received one of the most important gifts of the Spirit (12:28). In fact, they are placed third in importance after apostles and prophets. They form a special group within the community, for not all Christians are teachers (12:29). The letter to the Ephesians also mentions teaching among the ministries and gifts of the Risen Christ (4:11). These ministries and gifts are also mentioned in Romans—written to a church that Paul did not found himself (Rom. 12:7). In writing to the Galatians, Paul counsels that the one taught (*katēchoumenos*) should share all good things with the one who teaches (from the verb *katēcheō*).

We can only ascertain the function of these teachers when we read between the lines and feel the atmosphere in which they taught. The first important area concerned baptism. Most of the people to whom Paul wrote his letters were recent converts whose primary experience of Christian teaching had been their baptismal training. This formative initial instruction would give the converts the guidelines to follow all the rest of their lives. Thus the office of such a teacher must have been one of extreme importance.

This is confirmed by Romans, chapter 6, where we see the active place of the teacher in connection with baptismal catechesis. In writing to the Romans about the meaning of baptism, Paul reminds them of something that was very familiar to them as a result of their first instructions: "Are you not aware that we who were baptized into Jesus Christ were baptized into his death?" (6:3). Later he refers to the "rule of teaching," *typon didachēs*, to which they committed themselves at this time (6:17). The Christian way of life was rooted deeply in the form of teaching imparted during the baptismal training.

The second basic area of the teacher's concern—one intimately associated with baptismal instruction—was that of tradition. "Tradition" here means the "handing on" of the words and deeds of Jesus, in the light of his death and resurrection, and explaining how in these great events he fulfilled the Hebrew Scriptures.

For example, Paul explicitly states that he has received a tradition about Jesus that he has handed down to others, presumably when they were first instructed. He uses the Jewish terminology of tradition to describe this, first of all in regard to the resurrection: "I handed on to you first of all what I myself received, that Christ died for our sins in accordance with the Scriptures; that he was buried and, in accordance with the Scriptures, rose on the third day" (1 Cor. 15:3-4).

The same form is used when Paul refers to the teaching about the Eucharist (1 Cor. 11:23). Here we should note that Paul is not speaking about tradition in the sense of a system or collection from the past that is merely being passed on. The tradition concerns the *living exalted Lord* who is being proclaimed in the Eucharistic celebration (11:24-26). It is a Lord whom Paul has seen and experienced as alive (15:8). It is a *living* tradition that is being handed on.

This tradition, as we have noted, placed great importance on instruction in the Hebrew Scriptures, especially in regard to the manner in which Jesus "fulfilled" them. The expression "in accordance with the Scriptures" is used twice in Paul's tradition formula in 1 Cor. 15:3-4 which we have quoted above. Indeed, all of Paul's letters would have been completely unintelligible to Gentile audiences unless we presume that they had gained an extensive familiarity with the Hebrew Scriptures—a familiarity which must have originated in serious study during their baptismal instruction.

An equally essential part of the "tradition" concerned *how Christians should "walk,"* outlining a new way of life with Jesus himself as the model. This is the basic significance of baptism as a "joining to," literally a "plunging into," Christ in such a way that a person comes to live the new life of the Spirit characteristic of Jesus himself. In Rom.

6:4, Paul indicates that we were buried with Christ in baptism "so that, just as Christ was raised from the dead, . . . we too might live a new life." The Colossians are reminded, "Continue, therefore, to live in Christ Jesus the Lord, in the spirit in which you received him . . . growing ever stronger in faith, as *you were taught*" (2:6-7). Eph. 4:20-22 is even more explicit: "That is not what you learned when you learned Christ! I am supposing, of course, that he has been preached and taught to you in accord with the truth that is in Jesus: namely that you must lay aside your former way of life."

This focus on teaching a new way of life is strongly brought out in the fragments of baptismal catechesis[36] that we find in Col. 3:8-4:12; Eph. 4:22-6:19; 1 Pet. 1:13-21; and James 1:1-4:10. Each of these follows the same essential outline or pattern, making us suspect that they are drawn from a more ancient baptismal instruction. The pattern includes: (1) putting off the "old man," the former way of life, (2) putting on the new life in Christ, a life of virtue and worship, (3) praying and being vigilant against temptation.

Another baptismal text with a close link to Christian life is Gal. 3: 27-28: "All of you who have been baptized into Christ have clothed yourselves with him. There does not exist among you Jew or Greek, slave or freeman, male or female. All are one in Christ Jesus."

Here we see that one of the effects of baptism was to break down, at least in the area of worship, the great social and religious barriers of the ancient world. Unity in Christ meant a new unity with one another. The conviction that baptism meant a complete break with the past was built on the belief that a new creation, a new world, began with baptism, in which the old ties were no longer binding. This may have been influenced by the common belief among Jews that a proselyte's initiation into Judaism broke all his previous ties in the world, even the effects of blood relationships.[37]

The letter to the Ephesians also brings out the effect of union with Christ in baptism: to create "one new man" in place of the two previously separated branches of humanity, Jew and Gentile, and, thus, to bring about peace and reconciliation (2:15-16). There may also be a reference to baptismal initiation in Rom. 8:15: the Spirit enables a person to say, "Abba" (that is, "Father"). The Aramaic "Abba" would not have been understood by Paul's audience unless they had already known of the tradition about Jesus' prayer: that he used the same familiar term in speaking to his Father. The references to Spirit and sonship in the context make it likely that the converts, during baptismal instruction, learned to pray saying "Abba," just as Jesus did.

The baptismal admonitions in both Ephesians and Colossians concerning daily life and responsibilities may at first seem commonplace. But if we examine them closely, we will find that a new exciting dimension has been added. The authors call this acting and speaking "in the Lord." It was their special insight into a unique way of transforming the ordinary actions of each day, or of any person in any state or occupation in life. It did not matter whether one was a parent or child, a husband or wife, a slave, freedman, or noble. "In the Lord" meant that a person was so transfigured and transformed by the Spirit of God that he or she could be a shining, radiant, luminous vessel of God's presence and love in the world. The only important matter was to approximate as closely as possible the ideal of Christ himself and to become a humble loving servant of God who would simply allow the light and love of the Spirit to shine and manifest itself in every action of the day.

For example, "in the Lord" meant a new degree of intensity and excellence in every action because it became an opportunity and outlet for heartfelt love shown by humble service to the needs of others. Thus, the author of Colossians could write, "Whatever you do, work at it with your whole being. Do it for the Lord rather than for men" (3:23-24). This ideal would mean that a Christian would dedicate himself wholeheartedly, striving for excellence, to whatever work or profession he or she was engaged in. In the family, it would mean loving service between husbands and wives, between parents and children (Eph. 5:22; 6:1). This is summed up by the phrase, "Defer to one another out of reverence for Christ" (Eph. 5:21).

In community worship and gatherings, "in the Lord" meant an intensity of joy and devotion breaking out in community and individual singing: "Sing gratefully to God from your hearts in psalms, hymns, and inspired songs" (Col. 3:16). "Be filled with the Spirit, addressing one another in psalms and hymns and inspired songs. Sing praise to the Lord with all your hearts" (Eph. 5:18-19). In speaking with one another, it meant frequent enthusiastic acknowledgment and praise of God's work and intervention in their daily lives. "Give thanks to God the Father always and for everything in the name of our Lord Jesus Christ" (Eph. 5:20). "Whatever you do, whether in speech or in action, do it in the name of the Lord Jesus. Give thanks to God the Father through him" (Col. 3:17).

The letter to the Ephesians describes the whole baptismal learning process in terms of "learning Christ." The converts should be "imitators of God" by walking in love, just as Jesus walked, and gave himself up for men, even to death (5:1-2).

This same letter adds concrete details about the way in which members of the community should conduct themselves in regard to their conversation, their relationships to outsiders, their food and drink, their worship, their relationships between husband and wife, children and parents, slaves and masters (5:3-6:9). The convert is entering a community sharply distinguished from others in the way its members conduct their whole life. Here they would need experienced guides, as well as the help of older members of the community.

To sum up: *Teachers were all important persons in the early church, even though they are seldom explicitly mentioned in the Acts of the Apostles or the New Testament letters. They were chiefly engaged in preparing new converts for baptism. Here the principal concern was in handing on a living tradition about Jesus, showing how he lived and how he fulfilled the Scriptures. Since this tradition was embodied in the lives of the teachers, the teachers played an important part in training people for a whole new way of life which was like that of Jesus.*

# 21. The Spirit and the Community as Teachers

The New Testament writers were firmly convinced that there was really only one teacher in the early church, the Holy Spirit himself. Christians could be totally dedicated to helping and guiding others, but they were only instruments of the Spirit who alone was the effective agent of change that led persons to a new way of living.

As a result, as previously noted, there was a distinct fear of mere human discipleship in the New Testament documents. The name "disciple," except as applied to the followers of the Baptist, is never used of anyone except Jesus' own disciples. The early preachers of the gospel did make "disciples," but they considered them disciples of Jesus, not of themselves. This is why, in Matthew's gospel, the Twelve can only "make disciples" after the resurrection of Jesus when there are no longer any earthly limitations to his presence. Then it is very carefully specified that the disciples are not joined to their earthly teachers but are baptized or plunged into the Father, Son, and Holy Spirit. They are taught to be obedient, not to earthly teachers, but to the teachings of Jesus whose presence will always remain with them (Matt. 28:19-20).

Paul, as we mentioned, was quite disturbed by the attempt of some Corinthians to look upon themselves as his own "disciples." For this reason, he usually entrusted the ceremony of baptism to others, lest some might think this effected a bond between teacher and student (1 Cor. 1:10-17). Matthew, as we also noted, warned that the title of teacher belonged to Christ alone (23:8). He may have feared lest Christians follow rabbinic models of discipleship, where it was very important to state what rabbi had been your teacher.

Even in regard to Jesus himself, the early church believed that the same Spirit that gave power to Jesus' teaching was now present in them after his resurrection. The Spirit had guided Jesus in his actions and his teaching (Luke 4:1,14; 10:21) and now continued this same work in the church. Again, throughout the Acts of the Apostles, the author reminds us that the same Holy Spirit that was operative in Jesus is now working in the church. Consequently, teaching in Jesus' name is really teaching by the same Spirit that was in him. In the gospel of John, as we have indicated, the disciples are told that they will be able to become effective "doubles" for Jesus because the Paraclete, the Holy Spirit, will be teaching them (14:26). Paul takes special care to tell the Corinthians that their understanding of the faith was not due to his own words or any special human ability on his part; they were taught by the Spirit himself: "We speak of these, not in words of human wisdom but in words taught by the Spirit . . ." (1 Cor. 2:13).

The prophets had taught that in the last times God himself would directly teach his people. Jeremiah had written, "No longer will they have need to teach their friends and kinsmen how to know the Lord. All, from least to greatest, shall know me, says the Lord" (31:34). Isaiah had also stated, "All your sons shall be taught by the Lord" (54:13). In the New Testament, these prophecies are considered as fulfilled in the teaching function of the Holy Spirit.

This theme, that God alone is the ultimate Teacher of his people, is echoed by John when he quotes the above verse from Isaiah to show that the gift of understanding Jesus' teaching is one that comes from the Father (6:45). Again, in the first letter of John, the author writes, "You have no need for anyone to teach you, as his anointing teaches you about all things" (1 John 2:27). Paul may also be influenced by the prophetic theme when he writes to the Thessalonians, "God himself has taught you to love one another" (1 Thess. 4:9).

The Holy Spirit as teacher brought out results in his "students" that surpassed all their previous actions and astonished the people who came in contact with them. Before Pentecost, the disciples secluded themselves in an upper room in fear and intense prayer; they were afraid to go out in public. With the coming of the Spirit, they went out to the festival crowds and did not fear to speak openly about Jesus (Acts 1-2).

Luke calls this gift *parrēsia*, which in Greek indicates a new extraordinary boldness, confidence, or assurance manifested in their speech and actions. John had described Jesus as speaking in this manner (7:26; 18:20). Luke now sees this gift as continuing in the early church through the Spirit of Jesus. Luke notes that the Jewish leaders perceived this same *parrēsia* in Peter and John, thus recognizing them as having been with Jesus: "Observing the *self-assurance* of Peter and John, and realizing that the speakers were uneducated men of no standing, the questioners were amazed. Then they recognized these men as having been with Jesus" (Acts 4:13).

In other words, they experienced the same Spirit at work in the apostles that they had known in Jesus. Luke has a very special esteem for this fruit of the Holy Spirit. The word *parrēsia*, or the verb formed from its root, is used again and again by Luke to describe the speech and actions of early Christians under the guidance of the Spirit (e.g., 4:13, 29,31; 9:27,29; 13:46; 18:26; 19:8). Luke brings the Acts of the Apostles to a dramatic climax by describing Paul preaching the gospel in Rome, the world capital, in this manner: "With *full assurance*, and without any hindrance whatever, he preached the reign of God and taught about the Lord Jesus Christ" (28:31).

The Spirit as teacher in the early church produced a new phenomenon of spontaneity and creativeness in the Gentile converts. Individuals who previously seemed quite ordinary began to show new gifts and patterns of speech. The community at Corinth was not formed from the upper educated class (1 Cor. 1:26-29). Yet with the gift of the Spirit they began to distinguish themselves in church meetings. Some had the gift of tongues, others that of prophecy, while still others had the charisma of healings or charitable services (1 Cor. 12:4-11).

Paul's own life shows how he believed that the Spirit developed a real sense of independent discipleship among Christians. His greatest fear was a dependent type of relationship between a Christian and his human teacher (1 Cor. 1:10-15). In his own work, as was noted earlier, Paul was confident that he had one prominent gift—to be a founder of new communities (Rom 15:15-19). Paul was a traveling apostle; once he had established the nucleus of a Christian community, he traveled on and left other men to build on his foundation. Apollos was a man who specialized in that type of work (1 Cor. 3:5-7). Thus Paul felt that others had gifts of the Spirit that he could trust and count on. His whole object as an apostle and founder was to *make himself unnecessary* so that he could go on and leave behind an independent, self-supporting, self-governing, and self-extending community. Paul's example shows that the Holy Spirit as teacher intends to develop independent Christian persons, not subordinates or passive subjects.

At the same time, the Spirit did not work alone, but in and through a community of believers, making it "the body of Christ." Each member of this "body" was thus an instrument of the Spirit when it came to teaching others. From the beginning, a candidate for baptism would begin to associate with those already baptized and learn a great deal from them in the process. Here we might mention some of the New Testament texts which show that the community itself was a learning situation for personal and spiritual growth, especially through the love and concern of the community for all its members.

Matthew's gospel gives us a notable example of specific brotherly concern as practiced in the early church (18:15-18). Here is the case of a brother who, because of human weakness, has gone astray through some kind of sin. (A "brother" is not merely a title, but involves a close covenant relationship springing from mutual fellowship in Christ.) A fellow Christian should personally seek out the brother who was lost. If that fails, he should take along one or two other Christians in order to try harder to convince him. That failing, the whole community should make a final effort. The goal is not to attempt to "excommunicate" the person; this would only be a last resort to shock a man into seeing himself realistically. Rather, the aim is to do everything possible to help a brother in deep spiritual need.

In Galatians, we find evidence of a similar practice. "My brothers, if someone is detected in sin, you who live by the spirit should gently set him right, each of you trying to avoid falling into temptation himself. Help carry one another's burdens; in that way you will fulfill the law of Christ" (6:1-2). We should note the emphasis on humility and gentleness in these verses. The correction should not be in a condescending manner; each person should look at his own conduct and not judge others (6:1-5).

Paul's letters contain many admonitions regarding community life and practice which would have made a striking impression on a catechumen. For example, Christians should not sue one another in law court, but settle matters among themselves in a brotherly manner (1 Cor. 6:1-8). A love-feast or *agapé* should precede the celebration of the Eucharist, which constituted a weekly "continuing education" for the Christian. Here special attention and concern should be given to the needs of the poor (1 Cor. 11:17-34). The individual gifts of the Spirit are valued in importance to the extent that they are used to help and "edify"—that is, "build up" others (1 Cor. 12-14). As we have mentioned, converts must have been amazed to find that Gentile Christians, under Paul's encouragement, were organizing a collection for needy Jews in Jerusalem. This type of work, unprecedented in history, would be an overwhelming indication of the concern of Christians for their far-off, previously estranged brothers and sisters.

In Colossians and Ephesians we find special mention of the mutual teaching that went on in the Christian community. Members of the community should bear with one another and forgive one another as Christ has forgiven them (Col. 3:13). They are to teach and advise one another (Col. 3:16). The joyful spirit of the gathering will be immediately evident to newcomers as they hear the community ring out their voices in songs to God (Col. 3:16).

The impact of their close union in Christ gave rise to a new type of "ethic" that was built on a deep spirit of responsibility to fellow Christians. They are to be completely honest with one another in a spirit of truth because they are "members of one another" (Eph. 4:25). They should work hard, avoiding injustice and stealing, so they will have something more to share with those in need (Eph. 4:28). They are to be careful about their speech, avoiding evil talk, so their words may be instrumental in helping others (Eph. 4:29).

Finally, we may easily forget to notice the continual mutual encouragement offered by the personal sharing of their faith and their prayers for one another. When a Christian died, his "brother" should console the family and friends of the deceased by the faith in the resurrection (1 Thess. 4:18; 5:11). The "communion of the saints" was a deep sustaining force as they realized that fellow Christians were remembering them in prayer. Paul himself never wrote a letter without assuring his readers of his prayers and asking their prayers for him. A brother or sister who has strayed through sin should be the object of special prayer (1 John 5:16). This prayer was especially valued in time of sickness, when the family could call upon the presbyters of the church to pray, so that the prayer of faith would heal him. However, it was not only the presbyters who would be of help. Christians were to pray for one another and confess their failings to one another to be assured of forgiveness and mutual help (James 5:14-16).

To sum up: *The Holy Spirit was acknowledged as the real teacher of the early church. The Spirit prompted a new powerful confidence and independence in speech as well as in action. It sparked the development of unique individual gifts in the community while, at the same time, bound the members in close fellowship. Through trust in one another's gifts, it helped to develop each Christian as an independent leader. As the bond of love within the community, the Spirit made each person a teacher, so that the whole community became a learning situation for personal growth.*

# Part IV

# The Teacher in the New Testament and the Teacher Today

# 22. A Critique of the New Testament View of the Teacher

Part IV brings us into the world of today. First, we must make an honest critique of the New Testament view of the teacher. This is necessary because the Holy Spirit works in human hearts to the extent that they are ready to receive it and are open to the impact of its message. Through the centuries, the Spirit continues to give us new insights as to how far the divine actions can penetrate human actions. In doing this, the Spirit provides us with a critique of the past, even the New Testament.

Almost two thousand years have passed since New Testament times. These years have witnessed tremendous changes in cultures, world-views, and life-styles. The New Testament is not a static document from the past. It envisions a community that will continually move to new horizons under the guidance of the Spirit. The same Spirit moves us to look critically at the past and to build constructively for the future. A close look at the New Testament reveals the following weak points in its over-all view of the Christian teacher.

1) Most teaching was "male-centered." Jesus' first disciples were men, and all leaders mentioned in the New Testament, male. This was not due to the teaching of Jesus, but to the milieu in which the early church developed. It was a world in which women were in an inferior religious, economic, and social position. This fact, of course, has vast implications with regard to the position of women in the New Testament.

2) A second weakness is closely connected with the first. The "male image" of domination and power had a profound influence on teaching

as well. The influence of the Spirit never does away with the human element, and so we should not be surprised to find that instruction in the New Testament shows a decided tendency to be paternalistic. Male teachers, following the pattern of male domination in the family, stressed the importance of obedience, often, perhaps, at the expense of stifling individual creativity and personal decision on the part of their students. Even Paul did not hesitate to give direct commands to the churches with the expectation of exact obedience.

This tendency to paternalism resulted in a lack of sufficient attention to dialogue between teacher and student. Such dialogue gives opportunities for mutual growth as the teacher listens to and learns from his/her students, and as the students in turn are open to new communications from their teachers. The best progress is made when students have the opportunity to learn through their own life experiences. Careful listening on the part of the teacher can then help them to recognize, understand, and assimilate these experiences.

3) A third "minus" was the dim attitude of many early Christian communities to the world about them. Although Jesus himself drew much of his teaching from acute observation and sensitivity to God's working in history and in the world, there was a strong inclination to reverse this process among early Christians.

There is also little evidence that Christian converts were encouraged to become effective agents of social change in their world. Several causes account for what seems today such an obvious lack. First of all, the early Christians expected Jesus to return in judgment and power within a relatively short time, perhaps during their own lifetime. God would then transform the world and renew humanity by mighty acts of power. In the short time that remained, many Christians felt it was better to remain free and detached rather than to involve themselves in a world that was soon to pass away.

Further, there was probably not too much that average Christians felt they could do to change the great social abuses they saw around them—including poverty, slavery, and the subjection of women. It is possible that many Christians were not even alert to these abuses because they were so much a part of the culture of their own society.

Again, few of the early Christians were Roman citizens. Even if they were, it would have seemed almost impossible for them to change the status quo so rigidly guarded by the mighty Roman Empire.

This does not mean that Christians did nothing. They felt that the lordship of Christ should be manifested first of all in the church and through the church to the world. Consequently they directed their best efforts to living their own individual and community lives with such intensity that the world would be influenced by their example and behavior.

Finally, we should add that there was a tendency in some sectors of the church to regard human nature itself with undue pessimism. This tendency was due in part to the influence of Greek philosophy which regarded the human body as a corrupt vessel containing a noble soul. The truly Christian view, as presented by Paul, is that the contrast is between "flesh" and "spirit," not as separate parts of the human person, but as ways of designating the status of the whole person. "Flesh" means a human being in the state of alienation from God with all the weakness that this entails. "Spirit" means the whole human person as moved or "inspirited" by God. However, it was easy to misunderstand this description of the whole human person and to treat flesh and spirit as a dichotomy within each human being. Such a dualism could be a serious obstacle to personal growth if it hindered people from loving and appreciating the human body with its experiences and sensations.

This critique of the New Testament view of the teacher does not really weaken the dynamic picture that we find in the Scriptures. Once we are alert to some of the limitations of time and culture, we are actually freer to appreciate the relevance of the New Testament model for teaching and personal growth today.

# 23. The New Testament Challenge to Teaching Today

As we review the insights obtained from the New Testament view of teaching and the teacher, we can summarize the results and their application in the following points.

## 1) LEARNING THE WAY FROM A TEACHER

As we look back, we can see that Christian education must be a life-long process that begins right from childhood. Jewish education was very conscious of this necessity and gave special attention to the religious education of the child through imitation of his parents and through close participation in family and community worship. We have seen that the children's part in these affairs was even prescribed by ritual on such occasions as the Passover ceremony.

Any further growth and education was considered an extension of the process begun at home through imitation of one's parents. When Jesus accepted disciples, they were men who already had experienced at home a thorough Jewish religious training. Moreover, a number of Jesus' disciples—at least Peter, Andrew, Philip, and Nathaniel—were previously disciples of John the Baptist. This was an excellent preparation for their future work with Jesus. In fact, Jesus himself, after his home training, may have served an apprenticeship with the Baptist. It was by the Jordan with John that he himself was baptized and met his future disciples (John 1:29-51).

Throughout the New Testament we have seen the primary importance attached to imitation and example. This was not merely an external matter, but the assimilation of a whole new life-style from those who had already experienced it. A living tradition about Jesus was embodied in the lives of people who were following him. This way of life was based on love and intimately associated with worship and prayer. A living Way such as this can only be learned through close association with a teacher and others who are actually following it. Once this strong personal basis of "teaching" the Way has been established, other "teaching methods" such as story-telling, drama, and films can flow from it and strengthen it.

In the New Testament learning process, we saw the supreme importance of involvement and participation. Jesus and Paul did not teach through long lectures but through a type of "in-service training." The apostles of Jesus learned the meaning of grace or God's initiative of love, not from a textbook, but by accompanying the master as he went out to the sick, the sinners, and the religious and social outcasts of Israel. They experienced the kingdom of God as meaning a real sharing of material goods by living with Jesus in a type of traveling commune where there was a common purse to provide for their needs and those of the poor they could help. When Paul taught that the gospel was to do away with the great ancient divisions between Jew and Gentile, it was not a mere matter of words. He actually went around with a Gentile traveling companion named Titus so that people could see the first example of a Gentile-Jewish community in action. Paul was so convinced that the oneness and community he spoke of had to be a concrete reality that he even organized collections from Gentile Christians all over the world to help the impoverished Jews in Jerusalem. Association, participation, and shared involvement in action with the teacher are essentials in learning the Way.

Thus, by way of application, any group or class situation in teaching today needs to be supplemented by ample opportunities for such experiences. It is encouraging today to see, for example, various forms of "family-centered" religious education that are trying to provide not just instruction but living examples of people trying to follow the Way.

## 2) COMMON LIFE AND COMMUNITY, THE BEST TEACHING ENVIRONMENT

A real factor in the teaching effectiveness of Jesus and the early church was the "smallness" of the situation in which teaching took place. Jesus had a very limited number of disciples, perhaps originally only the Twelve. His type of work and approach was not geared to mass production. It needed intimate participation and sharing both in a life-style and in common action. The personal development necessary in educating mature disciples takes a great deal of time as well as intense exposure. This is only possible in a group that can come in close contact with one another and with their teacher.

*The church* in the first century was also in many respects a "small" church, with no church buildings. *The churches* met in Christians' homes, which could not have held large crowds of people. In a city like Corinth, there were many small assemblies or "churches" centered about one large house which served as a meeting-place. In such a situation, each person would come to know all the others and have the possibility of playing an active role in community life. (We must remember that a Greek household was not like a modern family; it included not only the family members but also hired employees—freemen—and slaves.) When any teaching situation is too large to enable the participants to know one another on anything much more than a casual basis, it is lacking a vital dimension.

All of this points to community life itself as the best environment for learning. The community of Jesus was a covenant-brotherhood as well as a fellowship in sharing his mission. In this atmosphere, the essential elements for growth, mutual responsibility, and care can be most effective. In both the community of Jesus and that of the earliest church, we saw that close community bonds, even to the extent of sharing material resources, played a prominent part in their lives. This consideration reminds us that without real community no authentic Christian teaching can take place. The church by its very nature is committed to establishing the kingdom, which means a world of justice and peace. It cannot merely *say* to the world, e.g., that the terrible barriers between rich and poor, between races, and even between the sexes, must be erased. The church itself must be a "scale-model" of the new world it is called to help create. Yet this "scale-model" cannot be only an exterior facade; it must be based on a deep interior transformation. This transformation can best take place in an atmosphere in which brotherly care and mutual help are first priorities.

Jesus did not have a life-time to train his disciples. He only had a few short years to work with them. Likewise, the early church leaders did not plan long catechumenates, impressed as they were with the urgency of time and the coming close of the final age. Consequently, more reliance was placed on intensity than on regularity in forming candidates for baptism. The "pentecostal" nature of so many of the early churches almost shocked a neophyte into change as he or she became involved in the life of a community which was deeply taken up with the presence of the Spirit.

We note this especially in Paul's descriptions of community gatherings at Corinth. He relates how an unbeliever could be so impressed with the spiritual gifts of the community, especially prophecy, that he would feel almost irresistibly drawn to make his own profession of faith (1 Cor. 14:24). Converts felt themselves moved by a powerful Spirit of God that enabled them to make new decisions about a change in their life-style—a change they would have previously considered to be completely beyond their power. Paul appeals to the Spirit itself as the effective agent of change when he writes the Galatians, "How did you receive the Spirit? Was it through observance of the law or through faith in what you heard? . . . Is it because you observe the law or because you have faith in what you heard that God lavishes the Spirit on you and works wonders in your midst?" (3:2,5).

From this we can readily see the need of reserving important time in religious education for intensive periods of prayer and reflection in a community atmosphere where some of the advantages of the "small church" can be realized. This may be through weekends together at times or through meetings in smaller groups where more time can be given to personal reflection as well as sharing on a deeper level.

3) "KINGDOM-CENTERED" TEACHING

The work and teaching of Jesus was "kingdom-centered." As we have pointed out in Part II, this meant that the goal and direction of Jesus' life was to create "shalom"—a world of peace and justice that would be truly God's world. As an instrument and agent of the kingdom, Jesus was not content with general statements or pious exhortations. Instead, he went about initiating the kingdom in a very practical and effective manner through concrete action.

The early Christians continued the mission of Jesus. Yet there was a certain transformation. They believed that the first stages of the kingdom had been ushered in with great power through the exaltation of Jesus and the gift of the Holy Spirit. Now it was only a matter of waiting before the final stage when Jesus would return in power and judgment to renew the world. The kingdom was *already* present but there was a *not yet* element also. Since the church was convinced that Jesus was enthroned in power, greater emphasis came to be given on devotion *to* Jesus, together with concentration on gaining new members for the church, rather than on the previous more dynamic notion of sharing *with* Jesus his mission to the world. The emphasis on new membership was also strengthened by a feeling that time was running out in history, and that there was an urgent need to evangelize the world in the short time that was left.

Despite the fact that nearly two thousand years have passed since the death of Christ, this over-balance on the side of "church-centeredness" at the expense of "kingdom-centeredness" has remained. In our own day, many Christians feel an urgent need to return to "kingdom-centeredness." Thus a teacher today would be more like Jesus himself in his concern for the world about him than many Christian teachers have been in the past.

We should note here that a return to a "kingdom-centered" teaching would quickly eliminate the horrible Christian counter-sign of division presented to the world by the hundreds of divided Christian denominations. This division represents the very opposite of the goal of unity in the world and in the church that Christ died for. A "kingdom-oriented" teaching would make possible a joint ecumenical training of Christians to which the various churches could give their best resources. Without a "fellowship of righteousness" brought about through working together for the kingdom, there can never be real church fellowship or inter-communion. Many people involved in youth ministry or work with groups of adults can bring this perspective to life within the limitations of their circumstances.

## 4) TEACHING THROUGH THE SCRIPTURES

It would be difficult to overstate the importance of the Scriptures. However, God's story in the Bible, and his story in the life of each person must come together to produce fullness of life. It is hard for the modern reader to understand that the Bible cannot simply be read as, say, the newspaper or modern literature. It was not written primarily to describe past events or people, but as a story to be *experienced and entered into.* This purpose is quite different from that of much modern writing which offers the reader merely an intellectual and academic exercise. For one thing, the Scriptures were not written for the silent reader to take in through his eyes. They were written to be publicly read aloud and *listened to.* In fact, the Hebrew Bible was *sung* aloud in ancient times so that hearing it could be a deeply felt experience.

The ancient Jewish way of "reading Scripture" was to identify as closely as possible with the story and to enter into it as much as possible so that one participates in the whole drama. For example, in reading or hearing about the giving of the Law on Mount Sinai, one should climb Mount Sinai with Moses, actually hear the thunder, see the lightning, and listen to the voice of God as addressed to oneself. Already in the book of Deuteronomy we see this view of past events. The next generation after Moses is not to look back on these happenings in terms of the past but actually to be at Mount Sinai with their forefathers: "The Lord, our God, made a covenant with us at Horeb; not with our fathers did he make this covenant, but with us, all of us who are alive here this day. The Lord spoke with you face to face on the mountain from the midst of the fire" (5:2-4). Thus, a most fruitful way to approach Scripture is to listen to God as speaking to us here and now. This is why

Scripture is best read in a deeply prayerful atmosphere of worship to a community of people open to its message.

The New Testament writings were meant to be read in this same tradition. For example, each of the three gospels describes how Jesus climbed a high mountain and was transfigured in glory before his disciples. The early church understood this story not as something only *about* Jesus, but as a story they could enter into by being transfigured themselves through the grace of God. This is how the apostle Paul appears to understand it. He writes of this glory of God shining on the face of Jesus: "For God, who said, 'Let light shine out of darkness,' has shone in our hearts, that we in turn might make known the glory of God shining on the face of Christ" (2 Cor. 4:6). At the same time, he writes that his experience is shared by the Christian through union with Christ: "All of us, gazing on the Lord's glory with unveiled faces, are being transformed from glory to glory into his very image by the Lord who is the Spirit" (2 Cor. 3:18).

To apply this tradition today, the teacher must make every effort to locate Scripture reading in an atmosphere conducive to this process of identification and *entering into*—that is, an atmosphere of deep listening, expectation, and prayer. The Good News must be proclaimed and listened to, not as words written thousands of years ago, or even yesterday, but as the words of a living and Risen Christ who is still speaking to us today.

## 5) TEACHING THROUGH HISTORY, THE WORKSHOP OF GOD

The source of Jesus' "teaching materials" was history itself which he considered the workshop of God. God showed who he was by the way that he acted in peoples' lives. For Jesus, "imitation of God" meant watching his work in history. This was in accord with the Jewish view of "study," which meant to study God's wonderful acts in the world about us. Since God is a God of history, revealing himself in human events, all of life was seen as the "class" of the great Teacher of the Universe. To "study" is to search for meaning in the events of everyday life and in the surrounding world.

The early church, like Jesus, was very sensitive to the fact that the world and its history was the workshop of God. Members of the early church listened to what was happening and responded. For example, when the prophet Agabus stood up in the Antioch community and announced that a severe famine was coming on the world, the community responded immediately. They decided that each person would put something aside for a collection to be sent to those most in need (Acts 11:28-30). This reminds us that the agenda for our teaching must be taken from the world around us, from what is happening here and now.

To place this idea of history as a "workshop of God" in a modern context we must transpose the biblical expressions into present-day language. Recently I saw a statement (I don't remember where) that read as follows: "When all of life becomes your teacher, then you become free from the pain that comes from unnecessary resistance and unnecessary desire." In the biblical viewpoint God himself is the Teacher. Every event, every meeting, especially the crises of life have a special meaning when we take that occasion to open our selves deeper to God's will and find what meaning it has in our lives. As we do so, we find a new energy and source of strength available (through the Teacher of the Universe) that enables us to grow personally even through what might seem to others only a loss or useless suffering. This process is truly liberating (God is a Liberator, as we have seen). It *frees* us from the pain of unnecessary resistance and desire in surrender to a much deeper underlying purpose and direction in our lives.

The teacher today, then, can find readily available "materials" in the lives of students themselves, who can be encouraged through daily journals or religious autobiographies to uncover meaning in their own lives. Both teachers and students can also use the daily newspaper to study the events of the world around them in the light of the gospel in order to see what kind of response these events might call for in their own lives.

## 6) THE AUTHORITY OF THE TEACHER AND CHURCH LEADER

A very significant "by-product" of our study of New Testament teaching is a much better perspective on the meaning of *authority* in the church, especially in teaching. The very word "authority" does not bring up a pleasant image when we recall examples of churches who have attempted to control rather than to inspire their members. It is refreshing to find a very different concept in the New Testament.

We have seen that, with Paul, *apostolic authority* is authority that comes from Jesus himself as the result of "hearing" the gospel and then presenting it to others as already assimilated and part of one's life. The seal of authority is imitation of Jesus and response to him. This becomes present in the life of a teacher to such an extent that his life forms a pattern that others can imitate. This type of "authoritative" Christian living is the only one that prompts others to listen and take notice.

In this connection, the concept of *tradition* likewise changes. It becomes truly alive when we see that the New Testament only knows a *lived* tradition that can be observed in the lives of a succession of teachers who carry on the tradition of Jesus. When they teach others, their students in turn become effective bearers of that tradition to others. Thus, it is not a tradition *about Jesus*, but really a tradition *in Jesus*, for he is the living one who is experienced in the life of the teacher. Paul would consider the best "teacher's credential" as the living gospel proclaimed in the teacher's life.

Apostolic teaching in this sense, then, is really the life-line of the church. It gives the church vitality in the world and guarantees its continuity in time. From a historical standpoint, this apostolic teaching gradually became centered in the presbyter-bishop leaders toward the end of the first century. Yet the primacy of the apostolic tradition and its origin from Jesus himself sets it above the hierarchy or any church leaders. Even where the latter have more or less taken it over (often regrettably so), the New Testament reminds us that the presbyterate or hierarchy is only at the service of this tradition to guard and protect it—not to control it.

All this has important consequences in the matter of choosing suitable church leaders. We have seen that the apostolic tradition is not something that can be studied or possessed by detached or merely objective observers. It must always be considered in its true nature—i.e., something alive only as it is lived out by persons through the power of the gospel. This makes it all the more imperative to select only those church leaders who are truly *teachers*, for it is only teachers in the New Testament sense who can be bearers of the apostolic teaching.

## 7) The Spirit as Teacher in the Church

The New Testament, as we have seen, was very opposed to the idea of mere human discipleship. Today this is again an urgent concern in view of various determined efforts to program personality and character development almost entirely on the principles of behavioral psychology. A deep conviction that the Spirit is the primary church teacher will help to encourage a variety of personal Christian expressions.

This truth has consequences for Christian teachers. As noted in chapter 22, Paul believed that each person has a unique gift through the Spirit. It is, then, the role of teachers to search for and develop this special talent. Thus they will enable each Christian to bring something new and creative to his/her community and to the world. Individual, community, and world go together because the Spirit is not a private possession—"The Spirit of the Lord fills the world" (Wisd. 1:7).

The role of teachers is *indispensable*, yet they become true teachers only when they make themselves *dispensable*. They do this by forming independent Christians who no longer need their former teachers. An independent person is one who is free and responsible for his/her own decisions. The teaching process involves the removal of the obstacles to this freedom so that each person can develop in a new uncharted way.

Teachers then have a humble yet important place in the church. They realize there is a God-given potential in each student that they must recognize and foster. To use the illustration of Paul: the Christian neophyte is like a garden that must be cultivated. Many people will work in the garden toward this goal. Some will water it, others will weed it, but it is God alone who provides the increase and growth (1 Cor. 3:5-9), thus providing true independence and interdependence.

# 24.  Women Teachers
# in the Modern World

In chapters 6 and 7, we pointed out the basic direction of Jesus' life: to inaugurate the kingdom of God on earth—a kingdom in which the great divisions in the world are to be broken down. Among these, Jesus gave special attention to the barriers between "clean and unclean" and other obstacles that kept women from their proper equal status in society. Although it did not act consistently in this regard, the early church did continue Jesus' approach in proclaiming that there was to be "no longer male or female" (Gal. 3:28) in the Christian community. Here we wish to point out three applications of this core teaching of the New Testament in regard to women teachers in the world of today.

## Leadership and Teaching

It has been said that religious education among Christians is something directed by men and carried out by women for the sake of children. While this statement is somewhat exaggerated, the predominate place of women in Christian education is everywhere evident. Yet so is the fact that women become an increasing minority as these teaching positions ascend in importance. As we move from elementary to high school, to college, to graduate schools, fewer and fewer women are found. Some college and university departments of religion are completely male. Most seminary faculties, both Protestant and Catholic, as well as theological schools, have a small minority of women professors, and in many cases, none at all. The same could be said about administrative positions.

The situation becomes further aggravated if we keep in mind that the principal and most important place of the teacher is in the official ministry of the churches. The majority of Christian churches, from the standpoint of the number of their members, still do not admit female ministers or priests. Even where they are officially accepted, females often find it difficult to discover a congregation which will accept them. When it comes to the number of women who have attained the office of bishop or other high-ranking position in church hierarchies (other than the Shakers), it would not be easy to furnish even a few names.

All this indicates that something has gone amiss. The church, by nature and definition, is the continuation and extension of Jesus' own mission. This mission is nothing less than the full establishment of the kingdom of God—a united world in which the great divisions among mankind have been healed. One barrier to this unity is the still fixed role of male and female. The church must not only preach the kingdom; it must embody it and present to the world a "scale model" of what that world should be. Hence the church must take special care to be an example in the area of women's liberation from an inferior status. It must first put its own house in order by acting to eliminate the subordinate place that women teachers have in its schools and organizations. This will only be accomplished when women are equally represented in the highest church positions.

In this matter, the churches need to examine their traditions carefully and remove all that·has its origin in a time-bound culture or theology. For example, the New Testament speaks only of male leadership in the liturgy and life of the church. This is quite understandable in an age where women could not have had the independence necessary for such leadership: at that time they were socially and economically bound to the household of their father or husband. However, independence is within their grasp today and, therefore, many people believe that the church should move, as fast as possible, locally and internationally, toward the complete equality of the sexes in the teaching ministry as well as in leadership in the liturgy and life of the Christian people.

Another reason why women's leadership has developed slowly in the church is the fear of sex itself. Where woman plays an inferior role in the family as almost a part of the household property, she tends to be regarded more as a *thing* than an equal person. Consequently, she becomes more a sex object and symbol of sex than an equal partner in a covenant bond. Commercial advertising has been quick to reinforce this attitude: the beautiful girl standing beside the brand new car is almost part of the bill of sale!

In the realm of religion, this attitude led to considering the woman as an "impediment" in those spiritual matters that demanded a man's full attention. For example, in the Hebrew Scriptures, men were not to approach their wives before the revelation on Mount Sinai (Ex. 19:15). It was customary for soldiers in battle not to engage in marital relations because they felt they were fighting a holy war (cf. 1 Sam. 21:5; 2 Sam. 11:1-13). Priests were expected to keep celibate during the time of Temple service because marriage relations disqualified a man from public worship (Lev. 15:16-18). This "impediment" factor was one of the reasons behind the high esteem for celibacy in the early church.

The church can effectively join the campaign against such views of sex and women by eliminating anything in its employment practices and leadership qualifications that presents a "male image" to the world. Where women teachers in authoritative positions are a distinct minority, they appear to be a peripheral part of the church rather than belonging to its personal core. The church should be a living sign to the world that the new age "where there is no longer male or female" (Gal. 3:28) has really begun.

## MALE-FEMALE IMAGERY IN CHRISTIAN TEACHING

It is quite evident that there is an overwhelming predominance of male images in religious teaching. The image of God himself is mainly drawn from an old culture of male superiority. For example, the father in ancient times was the master and lord of the family to whom absolute obedience was due; hence God is addressed as "Father" rather than "Mother" in most Christian literature.

Again, the predominant presentation and description of God in the Bible and theology has been in terms of power and control. God is mainly described as doing things that men usually did in daily life:

fighting battles, creating, designing, and planning. His strength and might lead people to awe, respect, and obedience. Images of love, mercy, and care, perceived as more typically "maternal," seem to take second place.

There is nothing, except our cultural backlog, that would hinder us from addressing God as "Mother." Indeed the Bible does describe "him" as acting with motherly care (e.g., Isa. 49:14-15; Ps. 131:2). Images of God such as those given in these passages should be emphasized in religious teaching equally with the father image, especially in teaching children. This practice would avoid an understanding of God as exclusively male. In fact, why not use the expression, "God, our father and mother" in public and private prayers?

It would be an equal mistake to present God as a sexless being who is neither male nor female. Actually, a very old biblical traditon presents God not as sexless, but as *sex-full*—as containing within his (!) nature the fullness and perfection of both male and female together: "God created man in his image; in the divine image he created him; male and female he created them" (Gen. 1:27). Consequently, God should be presented as embodying what is best in both man and woman together—qualities of caring, loving, and creativity. In fact, in praying to God as "Abba," Jesus was following a tradition of the prophets that portrayed God as acting with a tenderness and affection that combined the best in human mothers and fathers: "Yet it was I who taught Ephraim to walk, who took them in my arms; I drew them with human cords, with bands of love; I fostered them like one who raises an infant to his cheeks; Yet, though I stooped to feed my child, they did not know that I was their healer" (Hos. 11:3-4).

The same can be said about the male-female terminology often used in reference to the relationship between Christ and the church or individual person, e.g., bridegroom and bride. The marital relationship is certainly an xcellent symbol of love and intimate union. However, if it is used with the cultural connotation of a wife's duty to obey her husband, it is quite another matter. There are much better ways of expressing obedience to Christ than one which reminds women of the inferior status they still have in many societies. It is indeed beautiful and perennially valid for the author of Ephesians to write that husbands should love their wives as Christ loved the church and even gave his life for her (5:25). But when he states that wives should be subject to their husbands as the church is to Christ (5:24), he is using an obviously culturally-conditioned image, based on the subordinate place of women in the society and family of that time.

## MEN AND WOMEN TEACHING TOGETHER

As male and female images need to be used together in religious instruction, so also men and women need to cooperate in teaching on every level if the gospel is to be effectively communicated. Such cooperation has, indeed, already been initiated in many places, in diocesan, parish, and school staffs.

Again, the teacher is meant to be a reflection of God to those who are disciples. Since God's image, as we have seen, is both male and female (Gen. 1:27), a man-woman teaching team, either married or working in close cooperation, should be a less inadequate reflection of God than either a man or a woman alone.

We have, in fact, an example of such a team in the New Testament: Aquila and Priscilla, the couple behind the scenes who were to a great degree responsible for some of the successes of Paul the Apostle. They seem to have been already Christians, newcomers from Rome, when Paul came to Corinth. He lived in their home and worked at the same trade as they did. Their home became the central Christian meeting place in Corinth (1 Cor. 16:19). Before Paul arrived in Ephesus, he sent this apostolic couple ahead of him. When he finally arrived there, he found a small Christian community waiting for him. Not only that: they had converted Apollos, an Alexandrian Jew who was to have a great influence on the Pauline churches (Acts, chapters 18 and 19).

Encouraging man-woman teaching teams in all forms and on all levels of Christian teaching should, then, be a very positive means of helping people gain images of God including "womanly" as well as "manly" characteristics. Such teams should also serve as signs, however imperfect, of the oneness in Christ, and in Christ with God, to which the gospel summons us.

# 25. The Gnostic View of Jesus and the Teacher Today[38]

It is only in recent years that Christians are becoming aware that the image of Jesus as presented in the New Testament is not by any means the only image of Jesus held by early Christians. This great change began in the middle of the 20th century through findings of lost coptic manuscripts in a place in Egypt called Nag-Hammadi. These coptic documents (written in the 4th century A.D.) were translations of much earlier texts, going back to possibly the 2nd century A.D. They contained writings of ancient Christian communities with a unique view of Jesus and the world quite distinct from that in the New Testament.

A few years ago, an English edition of these works in two large volumes, called the *Library of Nag-Hammadi*[39] was published. Some of the best known of these books are the gospel of Thomas, the gospel of Philip and the gospel of Truth. These writings have often been called "gnostic" (meaning "knowledge") because of their stress on the need for personal knowledge and enlightenment. In 1981, a paperback edition of *The Gnostic Gospels*[40] by Elaine Pagels was published. Her work has made possible a much wider popular audience for the content of the gnostic library of Nag-Hammadi. Pagels' book was given a great deal of publicity and can be found in almost every bookstore. Equally valuable, with a more scholarly approach, is *The Gnostic Dialogue*[41] by Pheme Perkins.

To understand the beliefs and life-styles of early "gnostic" or "gnostic-oriented" Christians, it is important to sketch the world view on which they were based.

The Gnostic World View[42]

Characteristic of the gnostic view (as we have noted before) are the following elements, although there was no such thing as a universal gnostic teaching. Some Nag-Hammadi books have no Christian orientation, indicating Pre-Christian origins. Important for us here are the basic views of Christian "gnostics" on human nature and the universe that we live in. "Gnosis" centers on the basic conviction that each person (according to some systems; a select group, according to others) is a microcosm or little universe with the divine, the *pneuma*, locked within. However, most people are "asleep" or "drunk" and do not know about this. Consequently they do not know who they really are, and are unable to tap this powerful presence within them. This can only come about throught a special kind of inner illumination or "gnosis".

In the gnostic world view, there is only one Light or God. Through some kind of emanation of this light, the world came into existence. This emanation is described in some systems as a divine anthropos or primal man. However, in the process the divine man or emanated light became divided up, scattered and imprisoned in individual human bodies. Most gnostics felt that the human body itself serves as a kind of trap or prison for the divine sparks within that are part of the one true light. For the gnostic Christian, Jesus was a wisdom-type figure who came into this world to help us realize who we really are, and thus be liberated from the bondage of human flesh. "Salvation" would consist in an inner illumination or experience of the divine spark within, together with the "know-how" to escape the domination of hostile evil powers who had revolted from the light and held the world under their domination. Once they had learned to "escape" they could tap the immense powers of their divinity, obtain freedom and immortality, and be able to be united once more to the Light from which they came.


Jesus as Teacher in the Gnostic Documents

1. The authors of the four gospels were each concerned to bring out the true identity of Jesus and answer the question, "Who is he?" The central question in the gospel of Mark is "Who do you say that I am?" (8:29) Peter gives the partial answer in the words, "You are the

Messiah." (8:30) The answer has a more complete, confessional meaning in Matthew, where Peter states, "You are the Messiah, the Son of the Living God!" (16:16) In the gospel of Luke, Jesus is announced to be Son of God from the moment of his conception through the words of the angel Gabriel: "Great will be his dignity and he will be called Son of the Most High." (1:32) The gospel of John goes even further than this and identifies Jesus with the eternal word with the Father before the creation of the world: "In the beginning was the Word; the Word was in God's presence, and the Word was God." (1:1)

By way of contrast, however, in the gospel of Thomas Jesus is not presented as a teacher who comes primarily to tell his disciples *who he is*, but *who they are* because they are indentified with him and draw from the very same source that he draws from:

> Jesus said to his disciples: "Make me a comparison; tell me what I am like." Simon Peter said to him, "You are a righteous angel." Matthew said to him: "My mouth is not capable of stating what you are like." Jesus said: "I am not your master, because you have drunk and become drunk from the same bubbling spring which I measured out."[43]

In the gnostic texts, Jesus is indeed divine but he comes to teach us that we are divine, just as he is. This sense of identification is expressed very strongly in the gospel of Philip in which a follower of Valentinian (a gnostic teacher) writes,

> You saw the spirit, you became spirit. You saw Christ, you became Christ. You saw (the Father, you) shall become the Father. . .you see yourself and what you see you shall (become).[44]

According to the same author, one who achieves *gnosis* becomes "no longer a Christian, but a Christ."[45]

The inner divinity of the disciple is often expressed in terms of light. In the gospel of Thomas, the disciples ask Jesus where they should go. Jesus answers them, "There is a light within a man of light, and it lights up the whole world (cosmos)."[46]

Jesus' function as a teacher is to lead people to the inward path of looking deep within themselves to find out *who they really are*. In the gospel of Thomas, Jesus says,

> If those who lead you say to you, "the kingdom is in heaven," then the birds of heaven will precede you. If

they say to you, "it is in the sea", then the fish will precede you. But the kingdom is within you and outside you. When you know yourselves, then you will be known, and you will know that you are sons of the living Father.[47]

Jesus is the model of the person who has really come to know himself, and he asks the disciple to go through the same process. Those who do so become a "Thomas", literally a twin of Jesus because they find out that they are his exact doubles. Jesus' words in the gospel of Thomas are really addressed to the Christian reader:

Since it has been said that you are my twin and true companion, examine yourself so that you may understand who are you... I am the knowledge of the truth. So while you accompany me, although you do not understand (it) you already have come to know, and you will be called "the one who knows himself." For whoever has not known himself has known nothing, but whoever has known himself has simultaneously achieved knowledge about the depth of all things.[48]

2. In the synoptic gospels, Jesus works within the realities of everyday life in order to transform the world through a change in human relationships. He takes the initiative to call on the tax-collector, a much hated Roman puppet, to be a member of his inner circle of apostles. (Matt. 8:1-13) The violence and oppression of their harsh Roman overlords is to be overcome not by violent resistance, but by responding to their unjust demands by loving service; e.g., "Should anyone force you into service for one mile, go with him two miles." (Matt. 5:24)

However, in the gospel of Thomas and other gnostic documents, Jesus tells his disciples to avoid the world as evil, and shows them how to escape from it. The world is like a putrid corpse that can only contaminate and ruin those who touch it. In the gospel of Thomas, Jesus says, "Whoever has come to understand the world has found only a corpse, and whoever has found a corpse is superior to the world."[49] Disciples then should avoid or "fast from" the world: "If you do not fast as regards the world, you will not find the kingdom."[50] Jesus appears in the midst of an evil world, of people who are intoxicated and blind, not knowing their true condition:

Jesus said, "I took my place in the midst of the world,

and I appeared to them in the flesh. I found all of them to be intoxicated. And My soul became afflicted for the sons of men, because they are blind in heart and do not have sight.[51]

3. The gospels present Jesus as presenting a model of life to be imitated. "Follow me" is his first command. Specific teachings (Mk, Mt, Lk) are given in regard to the great problems of life: money, riches, power, marriage, prestige. Jesus' concern for social justice, for the poor and hungry becomes a matter of command for his disciples.

However, in the gnostic documents the important matter is *not what you do*, but *who you really are*. If you know who you are and are able to break away from th world, then your actions will all be good. Once people know their inner divine nature and are truly enlightened, then national distinctions, Jew, Gentile, Greek mean very little. Since distinctions in the sexes comes from the "evil" body, an experience of our inner divine nature brings about perfect equality, so that there is no longer a male of female:

When you make the male and the female one and the same, so that the male not be male nor the female female. . . then will you enter the kingdom.[52]

4. In the canonical gospels, Jesus is very concerned about human institutions. He blesses marriage, and advises against divorce. His disciples are a very definite and definable group of twelve, whose leader is Peter. Matthew especially gives importance to what appears to be a succession[53] motif: Peter is to be the rock of the church with powers to teach and judge in the same way that Jesus did. (16: 18-19)

In contrast, the gnostic documents exhibit a strong antipathy for all human institutions as being a part of an evil and corrupt world. Some gnostics even forbad marriage for this reason. The Jewish Law, as found in the bible is condemned because it commands husband and wife to beget children.[54] This is similar to the beliefs of those Christians criticized by the author of the Pastoral Letters, who writes that they "forbid marriage and require abstinence from foods which God created. . ." (1 Tim. 4:3)

Since gnostics trusted in their own inner light, we would suspect that they would distrust all external authority and teachers. The tractate on *Authoritative Teaching* in the Nag Hammadi library considers external shepherds as enemies. The only true sheperd is the voice of the inner shepherd heard through *gnosis:*

> They (the enemies) did not realize that she (the soul) has an invisible, spiritual body; they think "We are her shepherd who feeds her." But they did not realize that she knows another way which is hidden from them. This her true shepherd taught her in *gnosis.* [55]

The gnostic author of the Apocalypse of Peter pokes fun at church officials who claim they have special authority from God:

> And there shall be others of those who are outside our number who name themselves bishop and also deacons, as if they have received their authority from God. They bend themselves under the judgement of their leaders. Those people are dry canals. [56]

## The Christian Teacher Today—Does the Gnostic Image of Jesus Have Any Permanent Validity?

The Christian gnostic movement, first of all, is not to be lightly dismissed as a small splinter group of "far left" Christians whose ideas and lifestyles left no impact on the Christian Church as a whole. They were a numerous and influential group. The author of the letters to Timothy and Titus is addressing himself to a serious and widespread movement that has strong similarities to that of the Nag Hammadi documents. The "false" teachings are so widespread in Ephesus and Crete that the author complains that "all in (the Roman Province of) Asia, have left me". (1 Timothy 1:15) Irenaeus, one of the fathers of the church devoted most of his life to counter this movement and wrote his volumes, *Adversus Haereses*, in the 2nd century to attack their teachings.

What then can we take from early Christian gnosticism in Christian teaching today? I would suggest as a starting point that the gospel of John represents a very serious attempt to come to terms with the insights of Christian gnostics and present a compromise, or central meeting point between the "far right", represented by the Synoptic Gospels and the "far left" as represented by many of the Nag Hammadi documents. By "far right" I mean the tendency to emphasize the externals of the church, and the separation between man and God in contrast with a "far left" which emphasizes an inner experience and the divinity as found within human nature. Of all the New Testament writings, the gospel of John was one of the favorites of gnostic-oriented Christians because of its inner emphasis. In fact, the 1st letter of John seems to have been written to counteract in part the use to which the gospel was made.[57] And yet on the other hand, the gospel was finally accepted into the official New Testament Cannon by the whole church.

For the sake of convenience, let us compare the viewpoint of John's gospel in the four areas we have used above to outline the view of Christian gnostics on Jesus' life and mission.

1. Here we saw that in the gnostic documents, Jesus' concern is for an inner *gnosis* or illumination on the part of disciples that will enable them to know *who they are*, as people who draw their identity from the same source as Jesus. When they do this they will realize their own inner divinity. In the Gospel of John, there is more concern for *knowledge* than anywhere else in the New Testament. In fact, the verb "to know" is used as often as Matthew, Mark and Luke combined. The outside world simply does not know who Jesus is and who God is but the disciples of Jesus have this inner knowledge:

> Just Father, the world has not known you, but I have
> known you; and these men have known that you sent
> me. (17:25)

Living according to the teaching of Jesus means to know the truth, a truth that makes people free. (8:31) It is a deep interpersonal knowledge: "I know my sheep and my sheep know me in the same way that the Father knows me and I know the Father." (10:14) Eternal life consists of this knowledge:

> Eternal life is this: to know you, the only true God,
> and him whom you have sent, Jesus Christ. (17:3)

For other texts, and contrasts to the world and others, cf. 1:10; 3:10; 6:69; 7:17; 14:17. It is of interest that the author of the fourth gospel describes the believer's relationship to Jesus and God not only in terms of believing, but in terms of *believing* and *knowing*. Peter explains, "We have come to believe and *know* that you are the holy one of God." (6:69) Believing and knowing are also found in parallel in 17:8, cf. also 10:38.

Consequently, we see both in the gospel of John and in the gnostic documents a very similar emphasis on *gnosis* or knowledge. Yet in the gospel of John, Jesus is not only the *catalyst* of such knowledge but an intermediary. It is a participation and share in Jesus' own intimate knowledge of the Father. At the close of his farewell address Jesus declares, "I have made your name known to them, and I will continue to do so in order that your love for me may live in them, and I may live in them." (17:26)

In regard to the inner divinity of the disciple, so heavily stressed by the gnostic oriented documents, we find the closest correspondence in the N.T. in the gospel of John. First of all, nowhere else is the divinity of Jesus himself so clearly and sharply portrayed. Jesus does not hesitate to say, "The Father and I are one." (10:30) The crowds do not miss the implication of this statement and in the next verse some actually pick up stones to throw at him as a token of blasphemy. The gospel itself reaches its highest moment and climax in the confession of Thomas, "My Lord and my God." (20:28)

Yet the shocking statements about Jesus' oneness with the Father are paralleled by similar statements about the oneness of the disciples with himself and his Father. Jesus prays, "that all may be one as you, Father, are in me, and I in you. I pray that they may be one in us." (17:21) And again, "that they may be one, as we are one—I in them, you in me, that their unity may be complete." (17:22-23) Indeed the divine indentification with each person and each person's with God could hardly be expressed in clearer terms than in Jesus' last discourse when he says, "On that day you will know that I am in my Father, and you in me, and I in you." (14:20)

However, as in the case of inner knowledge, Jesus is described as much more an intermediary than a mere catalyst, as would appear from the gnostic documents. It is as a result of union with Jesus that the disciples receive the precious gift of oneness with the Father. It is a gift rather than part of their nature about which they receive an enlightenment. Jesus is the Way, the unique mediator through which the disciple reaches this highest point of earthly existence:

> I am the way, and the truth, and the life; no one comes
> to the Father but through me. (14:6)

Coming now to the Christian teacher, we see that the statements of Jesus about his own divinity have received abundant attention. However, there still seems to be a great deal of fear and hesitation about statements about the divinity of the disciple—perhaps because of the danger that these might be taken or understood in an exaggerated manner. Biblical statements about the weakness of human nature, and the need of humanity for God receive much more attention. More emphasis needs to be given to the God-like quality already in human nature, as expressed by the author of Genesis in the creation of man and woman. In Gn. 2:7, God breathes his own Spirit or Breath into them so that they share in the source of all life in a unique manner. We find a parallel to the Genesis text in John 20:22, where Jesus, after his resurrection, breathes into his disciples and says, "Receive the Holy Spirit." This is a fullness of the gift already given at birth. So it could be said that Jesus is an intermediary to evoke this fullness, which would be a position not too far from the gnostic documents. John writes, "The Word became flesh and made his dwelling among us." (1:14) He is not thinking of Jesus alone, but of the whole mission of the Word.

2. Here we pointed out that the gnostic documents have a strong sense of the world as evil. In fact, it is so corrupt that the only remedy is to escape it. This strong dualism is one of the basic features of gnosticsm. At first sight the gospel of John contains many statements that would seem to reflect this dualism. Jesus says to those who do not believe him, "You are of this world; I am not of this world." (8:23) Jesus' work is to bring judgement on the world, so that the prince of this world will be cast out. (12:31; 14:30; 16:11) Also, "I have overcome the world." (16:33)

The fourth gospel does have a very keen perception of the pervading power of evil, and of a constant struggle against its power. This theme appears right from the beginning of the gospel when the author writes, "The light shines in a darkness, a darkness that did not overcome it." (1:5) However, it is the insight of the author, as reflected in Jesus' words that this evil is not limited to an outside force, or a world from which we must escape. This darkness is within us. But again, this is not human nature as something which must be denied or escaped from as part of a hostile universe. It is a way of living and acting that is not in accord with Jesus' example and teaching: "I am the light of the world. No follower of mine shall ever walk in darkness..." (8:12) The biblical idiom "to walk" indicates a manner of living or lifestyle. Cf also 12:35,36. It is the deeds of darkness that are the enemy: "Men have loved darkness rather than light because their deeds were wicked." (3:19)

In fact, the gospel of John is careful not to attribute evil to only outside forces. In contrast to Matthew, Mark and Luke there are no exorcisms or casting out of devils in John. Satan is only mentioned as actually working through Judas, as an example of unbelief. (13:2; 13:27; 6:70) The only "exorcism" in the gospel of John is the "casting out" of the devil that occurs through faith, and through people being drawn to Jesus after his death. (12:31,32) See also 14:30,31 and 16:11.

The gospel of John is very concerned to explain the exact roots of these "deeds of darkness." These roots are the hatred and anger existing in human hearts that even prompt them to plan to kill Jesus. This anger and hatred has been present even in the beginning of the World, when it prompted an act of murder by Cain against his brother Abel. This is the inner work of Satan:

> The father you spring from is the devil, and willingly
> you carry out his wishes. He brought death to man
> from the beginning. (8:44)

It is because Jesus still sees this inner anger at work that he challenges the crowd with the question: "Why do you look for the chance to kill me?" (7:20; cf. 5:25)

For John, the remedy to this anger resulting in deeds of darkness is not to suppress it, or somehow avoid or eliminate it. The answer lies in open acknowledgement and responsibility for it. It means acknowledging that we are not free, but are in fact slaves of our own desires: "Amen, Amen I say to you, everyone who commits sin is a slave of sin." (8:34) The supreme disaster is not to own up to this, not to bring one's deeds to the light:

> Everyone who practices evil hates the light; he does
> not come near it for fear his deeds will be exposed.
> (3:20)

In contrast, those who acknowledge this, and take full responsibility for it, bring their deeds into the light:

> He who acts in truth comes into the light to make clear
> that his deeds are done in God. (3:23)

I believe that the fourth gospel has come to a remarkable insight in regard to the roots of crime, murder, hatred, violence and war in our world. The usual tendency is to look for causes outside ourselves and to place the blame or responsibility on others, on social conditions, political figures, etc. John would see the only answer as saying, in effect, "I am the world." As I acknowledge and take responsibility for all sources of violence as existing within myself, I am able to be freed from it and draw others with me in that act of freedom. For the author of

John, this is the first step in believing in Jesus and his message. In this way the author has avoided the trap of dualism in gnostic documents, as well as in many Christian works. The answer is not escape from evil, but rather "embracing it" as a part of ourselves, and taking responsibility for it. The inner search of gnosticism, it is true, finds the divine within each person. However, it is not willing to embrace the "dark within" as well, but rather attempts to suppress or eliminate it.

3. We have seen that the Nag-Hammadi documents have very little in the way of ethical instructions or directives. The important matter is to know who you really are, and everything else will flow from this. By way of striking similarity, the gospel of John contains no specific ethical instruction. Jesus' detailed instructions on marriage, divorce, riches and other matters in the Synoptic gospels are strangely missing in John. It would seem at first that the true inner knowledge of the roots of sin as seen in #2 above would be sufficient. And indeed this is an absolutely necessary first step. Yet John sees that once this step is made, a total and complete following of Jesus can take place. This is expressed by the constant and repeated emphasis on love.

This love contains every ethical instruction, and even makes them superfluous because it is such a complete and undivided giving of one's self. As a result, the gospel gives great attention to the quality of this love. It is so great and so consuming that it is a love unto death, a love like that of Jesus himself: "There is no greater love than this: to lay down one's life for one's friends." (15:15) It is a love that goes out even to betrayers and enemies as Jesus' did to Judas, his betrayer. (13:22-23) It is a love that manifests itself in everyday life by humble, loving service of others, even in such an ordinary task of hospitality as washing the feet of visitors:

> If I washed your feet—I who am Teacher and
> Lord—then you must wash each other's feet. What I
> just did was to give you an example: as I have done, so
> must you do. (13:14-15)

We can see then why Jesus would repeat again and again that his great commandment was summed up in the words "love one another." (13:34, 15:12) In fact this oneness and love will be a sign to the whole world that Jesus' words are true. (17:21,23)

Why then does John omit the specific ethical commands of Jesus and give attention only to the "command" to love? Unfortunately he does not tell us, and we can only guess with some probability of success. It is quite possible that the the author fears that some Christians might consider that their faith consisted of a set of directives or ethical instructions of Jesus as a type of new law. Thus their adhesion to Christ could take the form of an emphasis on the mind, or partial obedience to Christ. For John, the whole matter is total and personal. This may be why he gives so much time to Jesus' conversation with a woman (4:1-42), to his acute sorrow and identification with Martha and Mary over the illness and death of Lazarus (11:1-44) and to Jesus' personal feelings and love for Judas (13:21). For John, Christian living means "passionate living." It means total, undivided attention, love, and service to others that cannot be only a matter of external instructions and directives.

The teacher today can take confidence in such an approach by realizing that total openness and sensitivity to others really sums up and includes every ethical direction. This complete "listening" and entire attention is what gives zest and meaning to all of life. By such an outlook, the arts, whether music, poetry, literature, dancing or painting can be seen as an important part of the development of the whole Christian person. It is the same ears, eyes, and heart that give undivided attention and sensitivity to music and the arts that can be equally open to listen to Christ himself.

We have seen previously that gnostic Christians had little use for the institutional or external aspect of the church. In fact, they even made fun of church leaders, since they were so convinced that the only true church was the interior church they arrived at through inner enlightenment. In contrast, in the synoptic gospels, especially in Matthew and Luke we see a great deal of attention given to establishing a line of authoritative teachers as successors of Jesus. Especially Peter is most important in this view.

In the gospel of John, there is considerable importance given to authoritative teaching.[58] However, the emphasis is placed on the Holy Spirit or Paraclete that will dwell in the disciples' hearts and enable them to become effective "doubles for Jesus" in carrying on this work.[59] It is the Holy Spirit himself who is really the authoritative teacher.[60] John 14-16 is devoted to carefully establishing the line of continuity between Jesus and the early church made possible by the work of the Paraclete. All the previous statements in John about Jesus' function of teaching, and bringing people to decision are now repeated and duplicated by the Holy Spirit working in the disciples. Typical of statements of this kind are the words,

The Paraclete, the Holy Spirit whom the Father will send in my name, will instruct you in everything, and remind you of all that I told you. (14:26)

In the main body of John (chaps. 1-20, since chap. 21 appears to be a later added appendix), Peter is in much less prominence[61] than in the Synoptic Gospels. Andrew is the first disciple called, and it is he who makes the first confession of faith. Peter, however, is given the name of the rock. (1:40-42) At the end of the Eucharistic discourse, Peter makes a confession of faith as spokesman of the disciples, but this has already been made and does not seem to be crucial. It is only in the appendix of the gospel that Peter is given the shepherd's role, but the emphasis is more on feeding, nourishing and giving an example through his life and martyrdom. (21:15-19)

On the other hand, it is the figure of the beloved disciple who has more prominence in this gospel. He is the source of their tradition. (19:35) He is the one reclining at Jesus' bosom at the Last Supper, through whom Peter addresses a question to the Master. (13:23-25) This disciple is the first one to believe that Jesus has risen from the dead, even before Peter. (20:8) The beloved disciple does not betray Jesus, as did Peter. He follows him into the courtyard of the high priest and is even with him at the foot of the cross. These texts show that the beloved disciple is the special witness to whom the tradition of John's gospel is indebted. He is also the closest to Jesus' heart and affection. He is presented especially to be the model for the believer, who can be a "beloved disciple" by being as close to Jesus as he was, even to the cross.

By way of comparison, there is no doubt that the fourth gospel is close to the gnostic documents in speaking of the unique place of the Spirit as the authoritative teacher of the church. However, in contrast, there is no putting down or depreciation of the place of Peter, who must have been more important as a apostolic authoritative teacher to other churches. The placing of both the beloved disciple and Peter side by side in the gospel shows that a harmonious union can take place through such a recognition.

For the teacher today, the gospel of John provides a model of compromise between extreme positions. The first would be the exclusive insistence on the Spirit alone as authoritative teacher without recognition of the contributions that qualified teachers authorized by the church can make. The other extreme would be complete dependence on authoritative teachers that would make the rest of the church a merely passive obedient group that is not aware of the inner authority of the Spirit within them. What is certain is that no human teacher can possibly take the place of the Spirit and that all such teachers are real teachers to the extent that they are willing to let themselves and their influence over others "die" so that they may live with a deep freedom and trust in the inner guidance of the Spirit.

By way of final comment, the gospel of John presents a unique example of striving for oneness not by supression of but by recognition and respect for diversity. True oneness seems to be one of the principal goals of the evangelist's teaching.

The Jesus who proclaims, "I and the Father are one" (10:30) sees this oneness as a model for his followers. He sees a future in which there will be "one flock and one shepherd." (10:16) His work is to "gather into one all the dispersed children of God." (11:25) He prays again and again that all may be one just as he and the Father are one. (17:11,21,22) There does not appear that division among Christians into opposing camps that we see in 1 John, a later document. (cf. 1 John 2:18-19) In the gospel of John the more charismatic and deep feeling beloved disciple, is in dialogue with, walks (and even runs) along with the slower moving and slower to believe, Peter the Rock. They have respect for one another's roles, and do not resort to conflict.

# Notes

1. This statement reflects the view of form criticism that the gospels were placed in writing after their stories were used for a generation or more in oral teaching and preaching that was directed toward the specific needs and problems of the churches. The writers made use of this tradition, revised it, and also added materials of their own.

2. Cf. J. Jeremias, *Jerusalem in the Time of Jesus* (London: SCM Press, 1969), which has a special chapter on the Pharisees of that time.

3. *Aboth*, a reference to "The Sayings of the Fathers," is a Jewish collection of the maxims of the ancient rabbis.

4. B. Gerhardsson, in *Memory and Manuscript* (Uppsala: C.W.K. Gleerup, 1961), has a thorough treatment of rabbinic oral tradition and its methods. Cf. pages 157-162 in regard to stress on the spoken word and the prohibitions of written texts.

5. *De Congressu Quaerendae Eruditionis Oratio*, XIII, 68.

6. *Ibid.*, XIII, 70.

7. *Vita*, 11-12.

8. *Against Apion*, II, 204.

9. *Ibid.*, II, 174-175.

10. The descriptions of teaching in classical and hellenistic Greece are drawn from H.I. Marrou, *A History of Education in Antiquity* (New York: Sheed & Ward, 1956).

11. Cf. Note 1 above. The gospels wish to present Jesus and his disciples as models for discipleship in the church. Hence they may at times portray Jesus' relationships in terms that reflect a later period and a more developed faith.

12. P. G. Bretscher, "Exodus 4:22-23 and the Voice," *Journal of Biblical Literature* 87 (1968):301-311.

13. S. G. F. Brandon, *Jesus and the Zealots* (Manchester, England: Manchester University Press, 1967).

14. While I refer to the community as Essenes, it is not certain that the Qumran community can be identified with Josephus' Essenes.

15. Cf. the article of G. Kittel, *"Akoloutheō"* in the *Theological Dictionary of the New Testament*, Vol. I:210-16.

16. For a more detailed treatment of Jesus' voluntary poverty, cf. Buchanan, "Jesus and the Upper Class," *Novum Testamentum* 7 (1966):202-221.

17. Acthemeier in "The Origin and Function of the PreMarcan Miracle Catenae," *JBL* 91 (1972):206, makes the following observation, "Given, then, the epiphanic character of the stories contained in the catenae, it is clear that one of the functions of those catenae would have been to point unmistakably to Jesus as a kind of *deus praesens*, as one in whom the divine power is at work. In this first catena, he shows himself Lord over demons (5:1-20), sickness (5:25-34), and death (5:21-23, 35-43). In the second as one who, in his healing presence, does all things well (7:37, as the conclusion to the three preceding healings). In both catenae, he is Lord of creation, as shown in his mastery of the sea, and the wondrous provider of food."

18. B. Gerhardsson, *op. cit.*, pp. 163-170.

19. *Ibid.*, p. 134.

20. This is brought out by A. Wilder in *The Language of the Gospel* (New York: Harper, 1964), especially pages 9-25.

21. *Ibid.*, p. 64.

22. B. Gerhardsson, *op. cit.*, pp. 167-168.

23. For more information on Paul as a teacher, see D.M. Williams, *The Imitation of Christ in Paul with Special Reference to Paul as Teacher* (doctoral dissertation, Columbia University, 1967). Also, see my own book, *The Secret of Paul the Apostle* (Maryknoll, NY: Orbis Press, 1978).

24. This has been developed by D. Stanley in his chapter, "'Become Imitators of Me'—Apostolic Tradition in Paul," in *The Apostolic Church in the New Testament* (Westminister, MD: Newman Press, 1965).

25. For support of this view see *Christology and a Modern Pilgrimage: A Discussion with Norman Perrin*, ed. Hans Betz (Claremont: New Testament Colloquium, 1971) and T. Weeden, *Mark—Traditions in Conflict* (Philadelphia: Fortress, 1971).

26. Cf. H.J. Held, "Matthew as Interpreter of the Miracle Stories," in *Tradition and Interpretation in Matthew* (Philadelphia: Westminister Press, 1963), by G. Bornkamm, G. Barth, and H. Held.

27. *Ibid.*

28. Cf. C. Talbert, "The Redaction Critical Quest for Luke the Theologian," in *Jesus and Man's Hope* (Pittsburgh: Perspective, 1970).

29. For a fuller discussion of the place of Peter, cf. *Peter in the New Testament* (Augsburg: Paulist Press, 1973), ed. by R.E. Brown, K.P. Donfried, and J. Reumann.

30. Talbert, cf. Note 28.

31. For a full discussion of dating, cf. R. Brown, *The Gospel According to John* (Anchor Bible, Vol. 29) pp. LXXX-LXXXVI.

32. For a fuller development of this theme, cf. my article, "From Jesus of Nazareth to Christ the Son of God, A Newer Approach to the Genesis of New Testament Faith," *Bible Today*, October, 1972.

33. R. E. Brown has a comprehensive treatment of the Paraclete in "The Paraclete in the Fourth Gospel," *New Testament Studies* 13 (1966-67):113-132.

34. For a discussion of dates, cf. B. Reicke, *The Epistles of James, Peter and Jude* (Anchor Bible, Vol. 37), pp. 3-10.

35. For a wider discussion of the variety that existed in early Christianity, see my book, *Underground Christians in the Earliest Church* (Santa Clara, CA: Diakonia Press, 1975).

36. P. Carrington has shown this in his book, *The Primitive Christian Catechism* (Cambridge: Cambridge University Press, 1940).

37. For Jewish sources, cf. D. Daube, *The New Testament and Rabbinic Judaism* (London: Athlone Press, 1956), pp. 112-113.

38. This chapter has been taken from an article of mine with the same title accepted for publication in *Religious Education* (1982 or 1983).

39. *The Nag Hammadi Library*, translated by members of the coptic gnostic library project of the Institute of Antiquity and Chirstianity, James M. Robinson, Director (San Francisco; Harper & Row, 1977).

40. Pagels, Elaine, *The Gnostic Gospels* (N.Y.: Random House, 1981).

41. Perkins, Pheme, *The Gnostic Dialogue* (N.Y.: Paulist Press, 1980).

42. The most valuable study I have found useful for an understanding of the gnostic world view is that of Hans Jonas in *The Gnostic Religion* (Boston: Beacon Press, 2nd revised ed., 1963).

43. *Gospel of Thomas*, Saying )#13.

44. *Gospel of Philip* 61:29-35 in *Nag Hammadi Library (NHL)* 137.

45. *Ibid.* 67:26-27 in *NHL* 140.

46. *Gospel of Thomas*, Saying #24.

47. *Ibid.*, Saying #3.

48. *Book of Thomas the Contender* 138:7-18 in *NHL* 189.

49. *Gospel of Thomas*, Saying #56.

50. *Ibid.*, Saying #27.

51. *Ibid.*, Saying #28.

52. *Ibid.*, Saying #22.

53. For evidence of this succession motif in Matthew cf. Joseph A. Grassi, "The Last Testament—Succession Literary Background of Matthew 9:35-10:1 And Its Significance," *Biblical Theology Bulletin* 7(1977)172-176.

54. *Testimony of Truth* 29:30-30:15 *NHL* 406-407.

55. *Authoritative Teaching* 32:30-33:3 *NHL* 282.

56. *Apocalypse of Peter* 79:21-30 *NHL* 343.

57. For a very fine treatment of the relationship of 1 John, cf. R.E. Brown, *The Community of the Beloved Disciple* (N.Y.: Paulist Press, 1979).

58. It is authoritative in the sense that God is the author, first in Jesus as teacher-God, and secondly in the Paraclete, the Holy Spirit, working in the Christian teaching community. This line of succession is developed in the chapter, "John—Criteria for an Authentic Teacher."

59. R.E. Brown has made a comprehensive study of this function of the Paraclete in "The Paraclete in the Fourth Gospel," *New Testament Studies* 13(1966-1967)113-132.

60. Cf. note 20.

61. Cf. the conclusions drawn in *Peter in the New Testament*, ed. by R.E. Brown, K.P. Donfried and J. Reumann (N.Y. & Minneapolis: Paulist Press and Augsberg Publishing House, 1973).